WHAT THE DREAM WILL DO FOR YOU

Ever since I was a young boy, I have had an insatiable hunger to find the answers to two key questions:

- 'Why am I here?'
- and 'How do I achieve my purpose in life?'

These two questions have taken me on a rollercoaster ride around the world.

I believe *all* people have a calling and a unique journey that will allow them to realise who they are and how they can make the world a better place. This is The Dream.

The chapters and exercises inside will help you to:

- identify and achieve your life purpose, or calling
- identify and achieve your ideal career path (for all ages – including retirees)
- understand and develop effective business communication skills with customers and colleagues
- practice meditation techniques to increase personal happiness, concentration and memory levels
- overcome stress, and create a better work-life balance
- turn negatives into positives and create and sustain life-long relationships (business or personal)
- understand and utilise the laws of networking
- understand the value and power of a sabbatical
- identify and overcome debilitating thought processes.

I look forward to discovering our Dreams together!

GRANT RODNEY KITCHEN

THE DREAM

A PRACTICAL GUIDE TO ACHIEVING YOUR LIFE'S PURPOSE

GRANT RODNEY KITCHEN

RedDoor

Published by RedDoor
www.reddoorpublishing.com

HB ISBN 978-1-910453-52-0
PB ISBN 978-1-910453-43-8

A CIP catalogue record for this book is available from the British Library

Cover design: Megan Sheer
Typesetting: Megan Sheer
Illustrations: Joey Everett

Print managed by Jellyfish Solutions Ltd

The Dream *is dedicated to all the people in the world,*
passed and living, who have reached for the stars,
no matter what obstacles stood in their path.
For your courage, love and determination, I salute you

CONTENTS

FOREWORD

There are not many people who change the course of your life irrevocably. For me, Grant Kitchen is one of those people.

We first met at acting school in Sydney, Australia. The open and unspoken secret at acting school is that hardly *anyone* becomes a successful actor following graduation and most don't even really pursue it as a career at all. So it was with Grant and I. But unlike me, Grant was absolutely determined to find a way to make a living and a life out of his passion for performing and inspiring others, even if it wasn't as an actor per se.

So as I left acting school and returned to university to finish my economics degree and then find a corporate job, Grant was exploring alternative paths. This is something you will learn about Grant in *The Dream*. He treads his own path.

I remember the day he told me he wanted to become a motivational speaker. Motivational speaker?! 'What is Grant talking about?' I thought to myself. 'Is a motivational speaker even a thing?' There I was, working in management consulting, earning what I thought was good money and with good career prospects ahead of me. I was walking a sensible path. And meanwhile Grant was off pursuing some seemingly hare-brained idea. But Grant seemed excited and motivated. I was feeling unfulfilled and unenergised.

Grant could see this. So he pushed me to attend an NSAA (National Speakers' Association of Australia) meeting. I resisted. He persisted.

And eventually I relented. That night would change my life forever. I listened as two professional motivational speakers (yes, it was indeed a real job!) spoke about their businesses and their craft. It was as if the clouds parted and the angels' choir began to sing. For the first time in my life I could feel (but not yet fully see) a career path ahead of me that truly inspired me. I said to Grant: 'This is unbelievable. I can't believe this is a job!' Grant gave me a knowing look.

These days, I feel fully free. I feel like I am treading my own path and creating a future for myself and my family that I am truly excited by. I have my own business as a speaker and trainer working internationally with executives and leaders of some of the world's great companies. I am making more money, having more fun and feel more meaning than I ever dreamed I possibly could have in a career. It truly is a dream.

In this book Grant shares of himself and his journey so that you can benefit. In person Grant is uninterested in small talk. He always wants to talk about what is most important in *your* life and wastes no time in engaging you on life's big questions. So it is with his book.

If you have an open mind and the courage to reflect on yourself, your own life and your own career, I am sure that *The Dream* could be a meaningful step forward in finding your own path: one that truly inspires you and makes a difference in the lives of others.

Shaun Kenny
Founder and Director of People of Influence
www.peopleofinfluence.com.au

ABOUT *THE DREAM*

'In the middle of difficulty lies opportunity.'

– Albert Einstein

I believe the future prosperity of the human race would be assured if ninety per cent of the world's population tried to realise the true purpose of their lives.

Like all people, I've experienced triumphs and tribulations on the road we call 'life'. At the age of thirteen, I was diagnosed with epilesy; I also had a speech impediment and an obsessive-compulsive condition. I was an outsider at school, bullied by some of my peers.

I became an angry young man. Then, at the age of twenty, after consuming a lot of alcohol, I fell off a balcony. I was hospitalised and incapacitated for six weeks, before being discharged from hospital with a back brace. I was very lucky.

Over the next year, I reflected on my self-destructive path and my childhood demons, and with the help of a supportive network of family and friends, rediscovered the boyhood purity of hope, wonder and inspiration I'd lost on my journey to adulthood. I rediscovered the revelation which I now call 'the Dream'. 'The Dream' is a term I use to refer to my evolution through life, internally and externally. When we are children, everyone has a dream of how they would like their life to be when they grow up. It's hard to know how many of us realise those precise dreams, because they can get lost through our many life experiences – especially our painful ones. Hence, the Dream is both:

- Our childhood dreams
- And how we achieve those dreams.

THE DREAM – WHAT, WHY, AND HOW

WHAT: Your life goal – what do you want to achieve from life?

WHY: Why are you trying to achieve this life goal?

HOW: Through which life experiences, using your specific skill-set, will you achieve your life goal?

How many people throughout history have sung or written or talked about achieving their dreams? Dr Martin Luther King Jnr said it best: 'I have a dream!'

As I slowly left behind my destructive path, I became more conscious of the Dream with every endeavour I embraced. First acting, then motivational speaking and soft-skills training, then going on a pilgrimage to Santiago de Compostela, followed by a new life in a foreign country, developing my own business, and finally, becoming a loving husband. This has been my Dream so far, but the Dream is different for each individual. There are approximately 7.5 billion people in the world; therefore, there are 7.5 billion dreams in the world! This is how magnificent the Dream is.

The Dream is:
A practical guide to support individuals who are trying to fulfil their greatest potential

The Dream is:
A business book to help you realise your career goals

The Dream is:
A reference book to help you navigate challenging life experiences.

The programme in this book is a neutral process for all ages, and all people. It is for anyone who dares to dream.

HOW IT WORKS

I would like you to imagine this book as a toolbox. The first part will help you to realise and implement your dream; the second part highlights the hurdles that may sabotage your dreams.

The Dream is divided into two parts:

PART I: DISCOVER AND FOLLOW YOUR DREAM

The first part is designed to encourage you to analyse your life from different perspectives, while providing useful tools to confirm or ignite your life purpose.

PART II: THE OBSTACLES AND CATALYSTS TO ACHIEVING YOUR DREAM

The second part will take you on a very different journey. To use an analogy: the second part of the book is Darth Vader from *Star Wars*. It is the devil inside all of us; but, like Darth Vader, it is also your possible saviour.

PART I

DISCOVER AND FOLLOW YOUR DREAM

CHAPTER 1

DISCOVER YOUR ORIGINAL DREAM INTENTION

WHAT IS YOUR ORIGINAL DREAM INTENTION?

Your Original Dream Intention is what you would like to achieve in your life. It is your first conscious realisation about who you are, and how you would like to make a difference to the world. It is a lightbulb moment when you realise: 'Yes, that is me! That is what I would like to become!'. For many people, this has already happened, perhaps a very long time ago. Can you remember when it happened to you? What was your Original Dream Intention? What inspired you? Or maybe you haven't experienced this defining life moment yet? Your Original Dream Intention doesn't have to be limited to excelling in your chosen career. It is what you intend to do, and how you intend to act, during your time in this world.

Maybe you want to help people in a warzone or influence how people think. Perhaps, you quite simply intend to treat people as you would like them to treat you.

Nelson Mandela's Original Dream Intention was to abolish apartheid in South Africa forever. He was jailed and ostracised, but in 1991, he achieved his intention.

Your Original Dream Intention is the beginning, and it directly affects the outcome of your Dream. It is so important!

Firstly, we need to explore what you can do to identify your Original Dream Intention, if you don't know what it is already.

Think back to when you were a child: what were your goals? As you grew, did you have a burning desire to make your mark on the world in a particular way? If so, has that changed, or are you still true to those goals?

As a seventeen-year-old, I was inspired by how so many of my favourite Hollywood movies changed my view of the world for the better, and how they made me feel that anything was possible in my life. Even tragic films had redemptive themes where the central character seemed to learn something of great value. So my Original Dream Intention became:

to positively change other people's perspectives, or realities

It's vital that your Original Dream Intention is grounded in something that deeply inspires you.

So what exactly is 'inspiration'? How can you recognise it in yourself? Let's take a look at some synonyms. During my studies at performing arts school, the principal encouraged us to use a thesaurus to find verbs that would allow us to be more expressive. Ever since, I've found a thesaurus to be an essential tool.

Here are some synonyms for the verb 'to inspire', from Thesaurus.com:

- affect
- animate
- arouse
- be responsible for
- carry
- cause
- elate
- embolden
- encourage
- enkindle
- enliven
- exalt
- excite
- exhilarate
- fire up

- galvanise
- give one idea
- imbue
- influence
- inspirit
- motivate
- quicken
- spark
- stimulate
- sway
- urge
- get
- give rise to
- impress
- inform
- instil
- produce
- reassure
- spur
- stir
- touch
- work up
- give impetus
- hearten
- inflame
- infuse
- invigorate
- provoke
- set up
- start off
- strike
- trigger

Now let's look at some synonyms for the adjective 'inspirational':

- adorning
- beautifying
- civilising
- developmental
- edifying
- elevating
- enriching
- helpful
- influential
- liberalising
- raising
- regenerative
- uplifting
- advancing
- beneficial
- constructive
- dignifying
- educational
- enlightening
- expanding
- humane
- instructive
- nuturing
- refined
- socialising
- widening
- artistic
- broadening
- corrective
- disciplining
- educative
- ennobling
- glorifying
- humanising
- learned
- promoting
- refining
- stimulating

The purpose of the synonyms exercise is to help you discover your Original Dream Intention, and in doing so, help you to build a relationship to life and your own personal dreams. Now you have a good idea of what *qualities* your Original Dream Intention should have, the next step is to begin brainstorming what your Dream could be, keeping these qualities in mind and observing what inspires you.

Your Dream is the way in which you are going to manifest your Original Dream Intention in the world. In the About *The Dream* section I mentioned the WHAT, WHY, and HOW of the Dream. Your Original Dream Intention is the WHAT. For example, perhaps your Original Dream Intention is to change the way that people think. Therefore, your Dream might be to write a great novel.

A great indicator of an inspirational thought is what I call a 'feeling thought'.

It is important that you can recognise inspirational thoughts. Sometimes our mind plays tricks on us, and it is difficult to decipher what is real, and what is not. An inspirational thought can be identified through 'Feeling thoughts'. Feeling thoughts are inspirational thoughts that register in your mind and activate feelings in your body at the same time. For example, you have been headhunted by a recruitment firm with an exciting new job offer. The salary and work opportunities clearly exceed your current position. It is the job you have always wanted. Nevertheless, you are satisfied with work. You have developed a great network within the company, your income is sufficient to pay the mortgage and support your family, and you ride your bike to work every day. You have a dilemma! What should you do? Over the next few weeks, you analyse all possible perspectives but can't make a decision. You are in two minds: play it safe – don't fix what is not broken, or embrace this uncertain but possibly more rewarding work opportunity. One day the family portrait catches your eye as you sit in your office. Suddenly, images from the beginning stages of your career appear in your mind. The one bedroom apartment where you lived with your girlfriend – now wife, ignites euphoric retrospective feelings within you. It was an exciting time of growth and sacrifice. Both of you lived for the moment, but were dedicated to building your future together. You took risks and they paid off. During your reflective moments something happens, and a thought enters your mind and affects your entire body with unquestionable clarity. You have just experienced a feeling thought, and you realise the best path for your future.

There are no limits with your Dream.

Don't let 'ifs' or 'buts' limit your aspirations! Most people are afraid of failure and even more afraid of how they would handle success and all the challenges that might bring, but ignore what-if thoughts for now, and try to discover your potential. In later chapters, we'll talk about how to deal with the obstacles to the Dream that you'll encounter within your own mind.

'Nothing is impossible,
the word itself says "I'm possible"!'

Audrey Hepburn

EXERCISE 1: DISCOVERING YOUR DREAM

In the space below, begin writing short phrases that embody your Original Dream Intention and your Dream. Or, maybe, you can re-examine, reconnect with, and confirm the goals you committed to as a child? Keep writing, observing to see what inspires you, until your Dream evolves within you. Use a thesaurus. What do you want from life? How do you want to change the world? Acknowledge and embrace your 'feeling thoughts' when they arise.

CHAPTER SUMMARY

1. Consider what you intend to do during the rest of your time in the world.

2. A great indicator that a thought is inspirational is that it's a 'feeling thought'.

3. With your Dream, reach for the stars. Don't be afraid to think big.

CALL TO ACTION

Life is full of endings that are also beginnings. A new relationship or career or lifestyle also signifies the end of whatever came before. Are you closer or further away from the Original Dream Intention that you had as a child?

Your Original Dream Intention is the foundation for everything you create in your life. It is your direct channel of communication to life itself. Please be honest and responsible with your wish, and remember the time, place, and your intention when you make it.

ACTION STEPS

Step 1: Find a quiet place, close your eyes, and analyse or re-analyse those childhood experiences and visions that inspired you to make the world a better place. Your Original Dream Intention may not come to you straightaway. It could even take weeks. Don't give up! Break through all your 'ifs' and 'buts', and discover your dreams. To identify

Your Original Dream Intention, wait for a 'feeling thought' to arrive. You will know it has arrived, because it will feel undeniably true.

Step 2: Help bring Your Original Dream Intention into the world by writing it down with the aid of the thesaurus.

Step 3: No matter what happens: never forget your Original Dream Intention.

CHAPTER 2

YOUR DREAM CAREER – FOR FREEDOM-SEEKERS AND ENTREPRENEURS

At twenty-two, I was working in the hospitality industry without any clear career direction but with my love for Hollywood movies still fresh in my consciousness. Encouraged by my girlfriend, I decided to enrol in a performing arts diploma. Interestingly, most of my major career changes have been sparked by my partner at the time. Relationships with others are essential to achieving your Dream, as we will discover in Chapter 5.

I wanted to become an actor; I wanted to become a movie star, to be like the many Hollywood actors I grew up admiring on the big screen. Tom Cruise in *Jerry Maguire* and Tim Robbins in *The Shawshank Redemption* were two of my favourites. And I made the choice to pursue acting not with the idea of achieving wealth or security, but from the heart. The influence of my girlfriend and love for movies was the push I needed to take my first plunge into the Dream.

I remember my first orientation day at the professional performing arts school I attended for aspiring actors. The founder of the school was an American actor who had studied Method acting, also known as the Stanislavsky Technique. During his acting career in the US, Mr Gordon was named in the *Red Networks* newsletter, which identified alleged communists and sympathisers. After he refused to sign a loyalty oath declaration, he was unable to get acting work in America, and in 1952 he moved to Sydney. On my orientation day, Mr Gordon told us, 'Ninety-nine per cent of you will not have consistent acting work at the end of this course. If there's something else you'd like to do, then do it!'

Such overwhelming odds against success were intimidating, but they were also a challenge that made the Dream even more inviting for me. If the odds of success are low in your dream career, it can be a clue that you're making your career choice based on your Dream and not on your need for job security.

So, ask yourself this question. Was the number one reason why you chose your current career because:

1. You loved the idea of it and it inspired you; or
2. You were seeking security or money?

EXERCISE 2: ASSESS YOUR CAREER

Can you remember exactly how you chose your current career path – when, where and with whom? Pinpointing the exact situation will allow you to identify the honest reason for your current career path.

....

....

....

Was your decision more based on passion and self-belief, or security and money?

....

....

....

....

....

....

....

Note that although there are no right or wrong answers to these questions, the first reason is a good indication that you're following your Dream.

YOUR CAREER EXPECTATIONS

After three and a half years of enjoyment, heartache and pain, I graduated with a Diploma of Performing Arts. The next step was to find an acting agent to represent me in Sydney's performing arts industry: after several phone calls and a lot of door-knocking, I found one. I was on my way to becoming a Hollywood movie star! The Dream was materialising! – or so I thought.

After two months with my agent, I was making demands that he couldn't fulfil: I was working as a manager at a local Greek tavern, and my availability was limited, so I informed my agent that I could only attend auditions at certain times during the day – not advisable, because a young actor is expected to jump at auditions with vigour and commitment. The acting industry is so competitive, and actors who don't yet have a 'name' are at the beck and call of their agent and the casting agents. If you don't want the role, fifty other actors are waiting to replace you. What I was really, indirectly, saying to my agent was, 'I quit!'

Now, how is it possible I would do that? I'd just spent three years of my life following the Dream, challenging myself with a level of pressure that was beyond reasonable, in an industry with no guarantees. It didn't make sense to me then, or for a very long time afterward. Why would I put myself under such pressure only to quit?

Over the next year and a half, I was an angry, wild and unstable person, partying and experimenting with recreational drugs. I was angry with life for the situation it had put me in. It's clear to me now that I *expected* to become a movie star because of the blood, sweat and tears I'd already put into my acting studies.

Having conscious or unconscious expectations about your career can lead to severe disappointment.

When your career is under pressure from a ticking clock, you are limiting the creativity of the experience. Your conscious or unconscious expectations about your career can restrict the unimaginable natural organic process that the Dream already is – purely breathtaking, without boundaries. Only with a pure intention, and by utilising your specific skill-set, can you initiate a highly creative experience with your Dream career.

What about you? Use exercise 3 to begin exploring your expectations of your career.

EXERCISE 3: EXPLORE YOUR EXPECTATIONS

Do you or did you have conscious or unconscious expectations of your career? If yes, what were these expectations? Do you expect success because of your effort and dedication?

THE INTENTION BEHIND YOUR DREAM

After one and a half years of self-destruction, I asked myself, 'What do I want to do? How do I want to change our planet in a positive way?' So I revisited my inspiration as a teenage boy. I'd been inspired then by how movies changed my reality, how some of them influenced my behaviour for the better – and I realised that *I wanted to positively change other people's realities*. For example: as an actor, I wanted to challenge people's opinions of offensive behaviour. My thought process was: if I highlight the offensive character's pain and experiences, then hopefully, I can increase the perspective and the tolerance levels of my audience. This was the original intention behind my Dream, the reason I'd entered the performing arts industry. And a possible new path could arise from this intention!

No matter how much suffering you've gone through with your Dream, if you become lost, revisit your Original Intention and this will help to ground you.

HOW (ELSE) COULD YOU ACHIEVE YOUR DREAM?

If your current career isn't fulfilling your Dream any more, you too may find that revisiting your Original Dream Intention opens up other paths into the Dream, and reignites the Dream within you.

After a bit of searching, I fell upon a page that caught my attention: the website of the National Speakers Association of Australia, now called Professional Speakers Australia. I called the president of the association and explained my situation. It just so happened that he had also studied performing arts, and was empathetic. At the end of the conversation, he invited me to the next monthly meeting: so I went, and was intimidated and very impressed by the keynote presenters who performed. Most importantly, however, the Dream appeared to have been reactivated!

VOLUNTEERING TO BUILD YOUR SKILLS

After several meetings, I attended a workshop and told the facilitator that I wanted to start my own speaking business. He invited me to meet with him the following Monday.

When I arrived at the meeting, I got the impression that Doug's time was short. He advised me bluntly that I needed to write a keynote presentation, and explained, in quick succession, the steps I should take to achieve this. Then he told me I had one week to write it and bring it to him.

A week later, I was reading my first one-hour keynote to him. His response: 'Great! Now learn it!'

So I learnt the keynote verbatim. Doug then told me to sell it. 'To whom?' I asked. 'Rotary and Lions clubs,' came the reply. Rotary International and Lions Australia are not-for-profit organisations in which business professionals and community leaders volunteer their time, talents and resources to serve their local communities. Most suburbs in Australia's larger cities have a Rotary or Lions club or both.

After some initial setbacks and rejections, I 'sold' my first keynote presentation to the Rotary Club of Rockdale free of charge. The presentation was positively received – and I was on track to launching my speaking career! More importantly, I was continuing to follow the Dream.

Over the next two years, I gave more than fifty free keynote presentations to Rotary and Lions clubs around Sydney on the topic, 'Rapport building: the key to success in sales'. I also began my own soft-skills training company.

> You can create a positive environment of growth and opportunity by giving without expectation, rather than letting money, a short-term measurement of success, get in the way of the Dream.

Money is only one aspect of success.

EXERCISE 4: VOLUNTEERING IDEAS

What possible voluntary work-related activity could you perform which will benefit your career in the future?

THE DREAM AND PERSONAL SACRIFICE

By the end of my fifty-plus presentations, I had received my first corporate contract. I was being paid as a motivational speaker! The disillusionment of my acting career became a distant memory.

My personal sacrifice had brought great personal reward.

My speaking career was taking off, but I still attended PSA meetings, considering them an integral tool for my development. During one meeting, I met a business professional who would, several months later, become my girlfriend and the next catalyst of the Dream.

Joanne was a salesperson at a soft-skills training company, and she introduced me to her company's director. At our meeting, the director asked me to perform a keynote presentation for him so he could review my skills. Of course, I performed my rapport-building presentation, and an hour later I had a job.

The next two years were some of the most difficult of my life up to that point. Yes, I was now a professional motivational speaker/facilitator, giving presentations to corporate audiences at big multinational companies all over the east coast of Australia – but my personal life was in ruins.

This is important: as Ken Wilber explained in his 1979 book *No Boundary*, the Dream has no boundaries. While I'm focusing on career in this chapter, that's only one aspect of the Dream – it encompasses *all* our experiences.

Prior to meeting Joanne, I'd consciously wished for a romantic partner who would allow me to go forward in my career, and that's exactly what I received. However, Joanne and I began having personal issues at home, which were transferred into the workplace. Our differences of opinion at work were also transferred to our personal lives at home. It became very difficult, very quickly. Ever since I was a young boy, I've struggled with epilepsy, and during my time at the company, the constant personal and professional pressure triggered seizures or episodes. My body was breaking down.

Life can take you literally, so be careful what you ask for! Be aware of the purity of your Original Dream Intention and the wishes that follow it.

After working at this company for one and a half years, I was burnt out, and spent three months in recovery! I was back to square one with my Dream. Those three months were a time of reflection for me. The company offered me a lucrative training contract, but I declined, as my poor health meant that I wasn't in a position to perform the contract. I still expected that I'd succeed in my career after all the effort I'd put into it – but life then took a different turn for me.

I decided to embark on a journey, but in a different area of life. I would walk the Route of Santiago de Compostela, also called the Camino de Santiago or just 'the Way'. (I recommend the 2010 movie *The Way*, starring Martin Sheen, and directed by his son Emilio Estevez.)

PERSONAL GROWTH AND YOUR CAREER

The Camino de Santiago is an ancient pilgrimage, traditionally made to obtain pardon for sins. It involves walking 800 kilometres to the place where St James is buried, a town called Santiago in north-western Spain.

My intention, in alignment with the Dream, was to seek inward, personal growth. I had done enough outward development in creating my company and working alongside Joanne. Now it was time to open the doors to my soul and ask the deeper questions of life.

It was still aligned with my Original Dream Intention to positively change other people's realities: because in order to do this, I needed to discover the truth within myself.

The fastest way to follow the Dream and ignite your career is to embark on experiences that will help you grow as a person.

Over five weeks, I walked from Saint-Jean-Pied-de-Port, a small town in France near the Spanish border at the foot of the Pyrenees, to Cape Finisterre in north-western Spain. (In Roman times, Cape Finisterre was considered the end of the world!). I had some amazing experiences, but the one that stands out from the rest was meeting the love of my life, my wife Magdalena.

After finishing the Camino, I followed my heart and I went to Germany to visit Magdalena; we spent two romantic weeks together before my holiday visa ran out and I had to fly back to Australia. At that point, we had two options: we could either Skype for the rest of our lives, or one of us could pack their bags and move to the other person's country so we could start a life together. In the end, it was a clear choice. In November 2010 I left Australia to begin my life with Magdalena in Bavaria, Germany.

Yet again, a woman would spark a change in the career aspect of my Dream. And can you see how the aspects of the Dream interlink? Your career, personal journeys and giving without expectation are part of a spider web, working together directly and indirectly. Everything is connected!

Follow your heart, no matter where it takes you. Nothing is forever, and security can sometimes be found in the unknown.

As a self-employed business person, at the beginning of each year my income is not guaranteed. I do not know what I will earn. But through my belief in probability, and cause and effect, my income has increased exponentially over the last five years. I have found security in the unknown.

Finding security in the unknown can also apply to retirees in retirement. In Tim Drake's book *Generation Cherry*, Mr Drake highlights the necessity to remain an active member in society throughout life. His book is focused on the baby boomers generation (people born between 1946–64). Retirement can be a daunting experience into the unknown, but the Dream doesn't just stop because you are retired. What do you love doing? Voluntary work can offer a huge range of possibilities.

EXERCISE 5: A JOURNEY TO HELP YOUR CAREER BY EVALUATING YOUR SITUATION FROM A COMPLETELY DIFFERENT PERSPECTIVE

If you had an opportunity to take three months off from work, where would you go and why?

....

....

....

....

....

How could this journey bring clarity to your career?

....

....

....

....

....

FREEDOM AND HAPPINESS

I'm not going to lie to you. Moving to a new country and beginning again is not easy. I had to learn a new language, integrate into the culture, restart my career and make new friends. Yet for me, it's been one of the most rewarding experiences I've ever had. After learning German, I worked in Bavaria as a cook and landscape gardener to fulfil the requirements of my visa. However, I didn't lose sight of my Original Dream Intention and the development level I'd achieved.

I was learning German at a community college – part of a network of colleges throughout Germany – so, being a native English speaker and having a background in soft-skills training, I approached the school director to ask if it was possible to facilitate a Business English course. The idea was warmly welcomed and I began teaching Business English at two community colleges.

Within a year and a half, I had discovered a niche market in Bavaria: multinational companies needed Business English and soft-skills training for their employees. I reignited my company. The Dream was very much still alive!

Over the next two years, and after cold-calling many companies, I worked with eleven different German multinationals. I now have six regular clients. I have employed two Business English contractors, and administrative staff. I work from home, I'm my own boss and I love what I do. It's been a long road from the orientation day at the performing arts school, through public speaking at Rotary and Lions clubs and moving to a new country – but I finally found freedom and happiness in my career. This leads me to the final point I want to highlight in this chapter:

Following the Dream will not be easy.

The Dream doesn't allow ignorance to flourish – it tests your resilience and, in doing so, increases your awareness. You cannot truly understand freedom without experiencing its opposite. Achieving your Dream will take endurance, determination and non-negotiable focus on your Original Dream Intention.

My whole journey, from that teenage boy who wanted to become a movie star to being a business owner in Germany, was based on my Original Dream Intention – 'to positively change other people's realities'. And I now do that every day.

What steps can you take to awaken your career within the Dream?

CHAPTER SUMMARY

1. If you chose your career because it inspired you, it's a good sign that you're following your Dream.
2. Having expectations about your career can lead to disappointment and will limit your Dream.
3. If you're unsure about your career path, revisit your Original Dream Intention.
4. Give without expectation.
5. Personal sacrifice can bring great personal reward.
6. Be careful what you ask for in life – you might just get it.
7. You can fast-track your Dream career by pursuing personal growth.

8. Follow your heart rather than seeking security.

9. Following the Dream won't be easy!

CALL TO ACTION

Please know, you don't have to be a slave to capitalism. You don't have to find reassurance in statements like: 'I must pay off my mortgage; therefore, I have to work.' Or 'I have done this all my life, who would hire me?'

Through determination, self belief, and sacrifice you can create a dynamic career and use capitalism creatively. Know in your heart that you have a specific set of skills that only you possess. It would be a tragedy if the world doesn't experience you, in all your glory. When you discover your Dream career, you will be happy to work for the rest of your life.

ACTION STEPS

Step 1: Please sit down by yourself, and imagine a work situation where you utilise *all* your skills to their fullest potential. Where are you, what are you doing, what are you wearing, and how are others reacting to you? Please be specific.

Step 2: Now write down possible career paths that encapsulate this vision in your mind.

Step 3: Discover the right career path for you with a feeling thought (see chapter 1). Once you have discovered your Dream career, create a measurable practical action plan.

- What actions/tasks can you implement in order to ignite your Dream career?

- When will you complete these tasks? Please create daily, weekly, monthly, yearly objectives which are reasonable but challenging. Hold yourself accountable. Good time management is when you strive for long-terms goals – daily!

- Who do you need to talk to in order to complete these tasks? What will they receive from your task? It is important to create value for people. Also, how will they help you?

- How will you know these actions were achieved? What are the results? How will you feel when you achieve these results? What impact will your results have on others?

CHAPTER 3

VIPASSANA – EXPERIENCE THE TRUTH OF LIFE

From the age of eight, I've suffered from obsessive-compulsive disorder. My OCD has fluctuated over the years depending on my circumstances and stress levels. As an adult, I was desperate for a cure. The epilepsy I'd had since I was thirteen had also worsened.

I met an unorthodox general practitioner who helped me regain my health. First, he listened to my explanation of my current situation and the problems I had with epilepsy and OCD. Then he asked me to sit upright in my chair and listen to the clock ticking. This was all I was allowed to do.

I was incredulous, but did as he said. Immediately, my mind began to quieten. The sound of the second hand on the clock stopped the consistent dialogue in my mind. I suddenly became aware of what was happening within my body – I could feel twitches of energy in unpredictable and random parts of myself. It was like lightning in a thunderstorm, sporadic electric bolts lighting up the sky.

When I finished the session, my mind was quiet and I felt heavy. And I had no obsessive-compulsive thoughts!

I didn't know it at the time, but I'd just been introduced to a Vipassana meditation technique. 'Vipassana' means 'to see things as they really are'. It's one of India's most ancient meditation techniques, and has been taught for more than 2,500 years as a universal remedy for illness.

Now, how is this connected to the Dream? Well, what was my Original Dream Intention? It was to positively change people's realities. Would it be irresponsible of me to influence people from a questionable perspective? Yes. If I want to positively change people's realities, I need to understand myself.

Take a look at the diagram below, an illustration of the iceberg behavioural model.This model is a well-known tool for understanding why people do what they do.

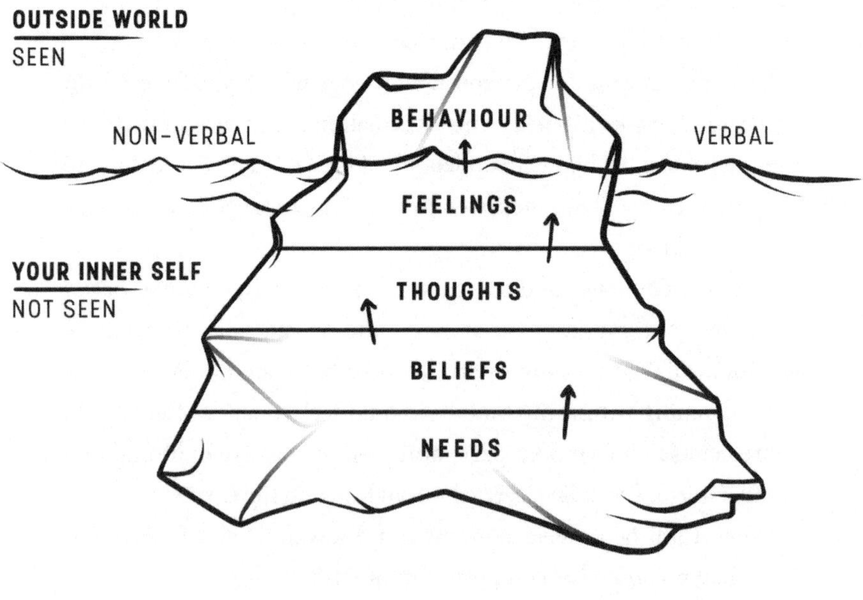

The iceberg behavioural model

As you know, we only see a small fraction of an actual iceberg, as most of it's under the water. The same is true for human behaviour: the outside world only sees the final result of a complex inner process before it materialises into behaviour. Have you judged another person because their behaviour didn't reach your own expectations? I think we are *all* guilty of this. But what are you really seeing?

Let me give you an example of how this works:

1. **Needs:** I need shelter to survive.

2. **Beliefs:** I need shelter to survive, but I'll survive more comfortably with a well-constructed house.

3. **Thoughts:** In order to build a good house, I need money; therefore, I need to be educated, so I can get a well-paying job.

4. **Feelings:** I'll feel more comfortable and happier with a well-paid job and a house that I love.

5. **Behaviour:** I'll enrol into university so I have a greater chance of getting a well-paid job.

Much of our behaviour is based on the needs at the bottom of the iceberg – and often we're not conscious of the reasons behind our actions. Vipassana meditation techniques help you understand these reasons and can also directly influence your thoughts and feelings. This investment in observing your senses will help you to understand the purpose of the Dream and the truth of your Original Dream Intention.

Your motivation is very important, but like the Original Dream Intention, you must let it develop for your Dream to materialise. In the same way, you might plant seeds in the soil so new flowers will grow, but you don't sit next to the pot and wait for the flowers to appear.

FOUR VIPASSANA TECHNIQUES

These four exercises to practice will help you explore your own motivations.

PREPARATION

I've suggested durations for each exercise, but really, timing yourself is unnecessary. Just concentrate as long as you can. Be honest with yourself and try to be disciplined.

All four of these exercises should be done in a seated posture. Find a comfortable place to sit on the ground, at home or somewhere quiet. Try to avoid lying down or sitting in a chair if you can. If sitting directly on the ground or floor is too uncomfortable, use a pillow or cushion.

The following diagram shows the three traditional sitting postures and hand positions. It's also acceptable to kneel while sitting on your heels.

SITTING POSTURES FOR VIPASSANA
WITH VARIOUS HAND POSITIONS

EXERCISE 6: MINDFULNESS

Once you're seated, perform each step in this cycle for five minutes.

Step 1: Begin to observe the sounds around you – the cars going past your house or the birds singing. Just listen, don't react.

Step 2: Now, bring your attention to how your body is touching the ground and how the different parts of your body are touching each other. Focus on the details. The longer you spend on each body part, the more effective the meditation.

Step 3: Next, go inside your body and, with your breath, send loving energy to each part of your body. Observe the changes.

Step 4: Repeat step 2.

Step 5: Repeat step 1.

Remember, don't react to your observations. Vipassana is all about not reacting – your aim is to become a neutral observer. If you begin to identify with what's happening in your body, the exercise becomes redundant.

EXERCISE 7: OBSERVING YOUR BREATH

Each step in this exercise should be done for ten minutes.

Step 1: Once you're seated, observe the transference of your breath from your nostrils to your top lip.

Step 2: Now focus on your right nostril only, and how the transference of breath touches your top lip.

Step 3: Now focus on your left nostril, and how the transference of breath touches your top lip.

Step 4: Repeat step 1.

The breath is the mind's salvation.

EXERCISE 8: VISUALISING YOUR CORPSE

Now, please don't feel weird about this exercise. The objective of it is to recognise that your body is not eternal and is constantly changing.

Step 1: Sit in the same position as before, and visualise your body as dead. See it laying on its back and observe the decaying process. Begin with the head and slowly observe each part of your body right down to the feet.

Allow your imagination to discover different decaying stages. See each part of the body changing colour, the skin peeling away, and so on.

Duration: Five minutes

Step 2: After visualising your entire body decaying, come to a place in your mind where your body has almost completely retreated back to the earth, then watch it *disappear*. What do you see now?

Duration: Five minutes

Step 3: Return to your senses and observe the sounds around you.

Duration: Five minutes

Step 4: Observe how your body is touching the ground and how different parts of your body are touching each other.

Duration: Five minutes

Your body is a wonderful instrument of experience and detection, but unlike the Dream, it isn't eternal.

EXERCISE 9: VISUALISING THE EXPANSION

Each of the first eight steps in this exercise should be done for three minutes.

Step 1: Visualise yourself meditating.

Step 2: Visualise yourself and your partner or a close friend meditating together.

Step 3: Visualise yourself, your partner or a close friend and your family meditating together. Where are you? What is happening to the world around you?

Step 4: Visualise yourself, your partner or a close friend, your family and all the people in your suburb or town meditating together.

Step 5: Visualise yourself, your partner or a close friend, your family, the people in your suburb or town and the people in your entire city meditating together. Where are you? What's happening to the world around you?

Step 6: Visualise yourself, your partner or a close friend, your family, the people in your suburb, the people in your entire city and all the people in your entire state meditating together.

Step 7: Visualise yourself, your partner or a close friend, your family, the people in your suburb, the people in your entire city, the people in your entire state and all the people in your country meditating together. Where are you? What's happening to the world around you?

Step 8: Visualise yourself, your partner or a close friend, your family, the people in your suburb, your entire city, your entire state, and the whole country, and all the people in the world meditating together. Where are you? What is happening to the world around you?

You can see where this technique is going. You can keep expanding until you have encompassed the entire universe or universes.

Step 9: Return to your senses and observe the sounds around you for five minutes.

Step 10: For five minutes, observe how your body is touching the ground and how different parts of your body are touching each other.

I want to highlight two points here:

1. **Your mind will try to do anything but meditate.** It will have you cleaning the car or jumping onto YouTube; whatever it can find. It will viciously procrastinate! That's normal.

2. **Don't be disheartened if you can't concentrate.** The capacity to concentrate is like a muscle, and you'll build stamina and endurance over time. Be honest with yourself and how long you can concentrate, and begin with short durations (as I've recommended) that you lengthen over time.

Vipassana will change your life, if you give it time. It will shine light on the different levels of the iceberg.

It's also been proven that Vipassana can improve other aspects of your life and health, as it contributes to a more formidable immune system and better mental health.

We live in a world of quick fixes! When we have a headache, we take a headache tablet, if our muscles ache, we rub cream to soothe the pain, but do we really resolve the problem? I have met with neurological doctors for many years because of my OCD and epilepsy. Unfortunately, the doctors do not have the capacity to resolve my problems. Their medicine is too limited to explore my thoughts and mind. They can only offer me band-aid solutions. Drugs! But with Vipassana you can directly influence your thoughts and feelings. This investment in concentrating and observing your senses will give you much needed respite from your increasingly demanding work life. Vipassana doesn't only give you fantastic work-life balance, but it can also unveil the many mysteries in your mind and body.

I know it isn't easy, but try and make these exercises a habit – the rewards are beyond your imagination. An optimum routine would involve meditating for two to three hours a week.

CHAPTER SUMMARY

1. The aim in Vipassana is to be a neutral observer – to not react.

2. Remember that the breath is the mind's salvation.

3. Your body isn't eternal.

4. It's normal for your mind to try to avoid meditating.

5. Your capacity to concentrate can be built over time, so don't be disheartened.

6. Vipassana can boost your immunity and mental health, as well as helping you to understand the hidden levels of your personal 'icebergs'.

CALL TO ACTION

Vipassana is the doorway to understand the limitations and potential of the most complex organism on earth – the human mind! It can unveil the many mysteries of life, give you wisdom, heal and protect you from illness.

Are you ready to increase your awareness, overcome suffering, and understand the statement: 'living in the now'?

ACTION STEPS

Step 1: Get hold of a comfortable meditation beanbag cushion. Choose what best suits you. Preferably, the beanbag cushion should be firm – 10-15 cm in height, so your legs can touch the ground comfortably. Meditating without a beanbag is ideal, but for beginners, the beanbag is essential.

Step 2: Please allocate thirty minutes in time in your schedule just for you. Find a quiet corner in your house or apartment where you can't be disturbed.

Step 3: For your first sitting, begin with exercise 6. Then slowly rotate each exercise through your other sittings. I personally begin every sitting with exercise 6, then I move through the other exercises.

Special note: This is your experience. Use your intuition to find what exercises work for you. Be honest with yourself, and always try to push your concentration a little bit further in each sitting. Please do not be disheartened if you cannot meditate on particular days, or if you cannot concentrate for a long time. Your brain needs time to strengthen its resilience from the effects of its own thoughts. Be patient, and observe your awareness after each sitting.

CHAPTER 4

UNDERSTANDING OPPOSITES – HOW TO TURN NEGATIVES INTO POSITIVES

There is an important life rule that both limits and allows the Dream to express its infinite creativity.

During one meeting with my unorthodox doctor, he drew the following diagram:

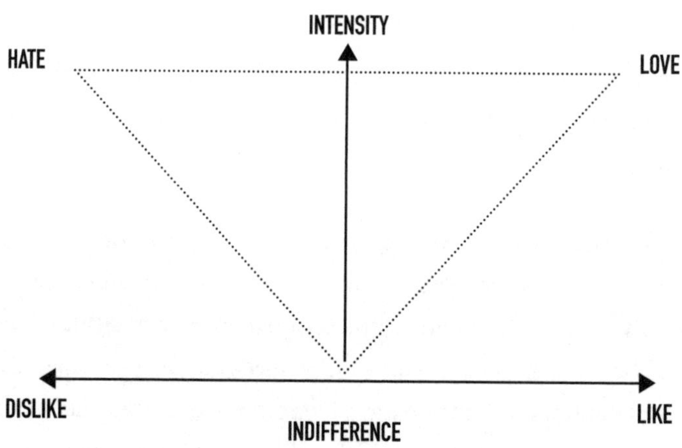

He then used it to explain how the universe began.

In Stephen Hawking's book *A Brief History of Time*, Hawking discusses the big bang theory – the currently accepted scientific explanation of the beginning of the universe. Even some religious communities, like the Catholic Church, now accept this explanation.

So, the 'indifference' line in the figure is the big bang, which occurred approximately 14 billion years ago. According to my doctor, a separation was created during the big bang which produced *opposites*. These positive and negative opposites – 'dislike' and 'like', and 'hate' and 'love' – can be seen in the diagram. These opposites do not work together harmoniously, even though they all come from the 'indifference' point in the centre. Each opposite contradicts the other.

Let's take a look at a few more examples.

OPPOSITES		
absent	....	present
abundant	....	scarce
man	....	woman
to be	....	not to be
blame	....	praise
bless	....	curse
bitter	....	sweet
heaven	....	hell
heavy	....	light
help	....	hinder
happy	....	sad
polite	....	rude, impolite
possible	....	impossible

My question to you is: can you have one opposite without the other? Can there be 'being' without 'not being'? Can something be deemed heavy without there being lighter things to compare it to? No. Opposites can't exist without each other, even though they're opposites. This means, even though it may be difficult to accept, that a world with love is also a world that has hate.

Derm Barrett's 1998 book *The Paradox Process: creative business solutions…where you least expect to find them* explains the creative process behind this phenomenon. It's a must-read for its insight into paradoxes and the different thought processes behind pairs of opposites.

In life, we sometimes experience the kind of hardship that can bring us to the brink of despair. We may suffer from many different types of illnesses over our lifetimes, and at some point we all die. When we receive difficult news, our first reaction is shock, then we attempt to find meaning in it. This response may then turn into anger and sometimes violence.

Just look at the world around you and notice how many negative mental processes have manifested into negative behaviour. It's everywhere! Now, what if I told you that such negative reactions could be avoided? Do you think it's possible to react positively in every situation and ensure that negative behaviours don't eventually come to the fore?

Malala Yousafzai, a Pakistani activist who was seriously injured by a Taliban gunman, held on to her life, overcame unconsciousness and intensive care to become the co-recipient of the 2014 Nobel Peace Prize. Ms Yousafzai has also co-authored her own book *I am Malala*, an international bestseller, founded her own non-profit organisation, the Malala Fund, and in *Time* magazine (2013-15) was voted one of the most influentical people globally.

It is possible to overcome hardship and turn negatives into positives. Through our creative minds, we can transform ALL destructive experiences and create positive outcomes for ourselves and others.

TURNING A NEGATIVE INTO A POSITIVE: MY ENGAGEMENT STORY

In 2015, I was informed by the German government that I had breached my visa requirements, and that if I didn't respond to their visa termination letter within ten days I'd be sent back to Australia and unable to enter Germany again for a year.

Initially, this news was heartbreaking for us. After all the work we'd put into creating a life together in Germany, it might now come to an end! We consulted our immigration lawyer, however, and discovered that there was a way I could stay in the country: Magdalena and I could marry. Now we had to face the facts: we either got married or we separated.

I found myself at a crossroads, confronted by a man inside of me. I knew who he was, but had never acknowledged him before. He was the 'single man' part of me, a part that didn't want to commit to anything or anyone and was always keeping his eyes open for the next possibility. It dawned on me that this 'single man' was the only reason I hadn't yet asked Magdalena to marry me. It wasn't the German immigration department dictating terms to us – it was the 'single man'!

The following day was a day from the gods, with the sun shining and everything sharp and clear. As we hiked up the mountain, Magdalena was fifteen metres ahead of me, and reached the top first. As I approached her, I just went for it – I got down on one knee and asked, 'Will you marry me?' Luckily, she said 'Yes'!

The next week my visa deadline arrived, but something very interesting happened: Magdalena and I were handed a lifeline from the German immigration department. I was advised to fly to the UK for twenty-four hours, then return to Germany as a visitor and apply for a new visa. I was told that I wouldn't have a problem with my new visa application.

This was a 180-degree turnaround from the letter I had received ten days before! The following week Magdalena and I flew to the UK for a day. During my new visa registration meeting in Germany, I was told in no uncertain terms that I wouldn't be able to work while the application was being processed.

'But I have a business,' I pleaded.

'No. You cannot work, Mr Kitchen, or you will be sent back to Australia.'

Now, let's look at this situation in terms of opposites:

The negative: I received difficult news that could have jeopardised my relationship with Magdalena.

On the other hand, positives sprang from this initial negative news – I confronted and overcame the 'single man' inside of me, Magdalena and I would marry and hence commit to spending the rest of our lives together, and we could continue in Germany under a new visa.

The second negative: I wouldn't be able to work while the application was being processed.

The positive: Not being able to work meant that I had time to write this book!

From one 'negative' letter and an unreasonable immigration officer, I had made several positive, life-changing decisions.

In every situation, opposites exist. Your task is to recognise each opposite in a situation and allow the 'positive opposite' to manifest.

Wayne Bennett, the most successful rugby league coach in Australian history, once said, 'If you create a positive culture within the team, then that's what you will have, a positive culture.' The opposites feed off themselves: one negative thought turns into a bigger negative thought, which turns into an even bigger negative thought. Bennett tells a cherokee story about the battle between two wolves, who represent the battles inside of us. One wolf is anger, envy, jealousy, sorrow, regret, greed, arrogance, self-pity, guilt, resentment, inferiority, lies, false pride, superiority, and ego. The other wolf is joy, peace, love, hope, sincerity, humility, kindness, benevolence, empathy, generosity, truth, compassion, and faith. Which wolf wins? The one you feed. 'Which wolf are you feeding?' Wayne Bennett asks.

> Negatives can only continue to exist when they're fuelled by negative thoughts.

Try to remember this the next time you are complaining about a situation or a person that habitually bothers you. Instead, focus on better self-care and stop giving that situation or person your precious energy. The more you complain, the further you move away from your objective – to resolve the unpleasant feelings inside of you.

HOW TO RECONCILE OPPOSITES: PARADOXES

The two opposites reconcile through contradictions, or *paradoxes*. For example:

I wanted to marry Magdalena on my own terms.

We ended up deciding to marry because of the immigration department's visa termination letter.

I was told I could work in Germany without marrying Magdalena, but we decided to get married anyway.

In order to turn a disaster into a triumph, you must try to reconcile the opposites.

How do you do that? Well, it's not an easy process, especially when the negatives can be so overwhelming, but let's try.

The first logical step is to look for the positive in each and every situation where you feel only negatives exist. Please don't allow yourself to say, 'There's no positive in this situation!' There's a positive and a negative in every situation, and you have a choice. You can either:

1. Focus on the pain and disappointment from the 'negative opposite', or

2. Focus on the positive *and* negative opposites, and allow the two opposites to reconcile and find a solution.

Remember, the opposites feed off themselves – off negative or positive thoughts. So, in order to manifest a positive solution, you must be positive, while at the same time trying to understand the reason for the negative.

When you choose to focus on and react to the positive opposite, it will grow and build its own momentum.

The Dream will not be easy at times – it may even break you. But if you can identify every positive in each situation, you are closer to achieving your dreams. Try it now in the following exercise.

EXERCISE 10: RECONCILING OPPOSITES IN YOUR PERSONAL LIFE

Describe a current personal situation that seems to be getting worse.

What's your current opinion of the situation? Please write down your negative and positive thoughts overleaf. Be honest with yourself.

NEGATIVE THOUGHTS	POSITIVE THOUGHTS

Now, re-read every thought you wrote in the negative column. If you haven't written a positive thought to counter every negative thought, re-evaluate that. Dig deep within yourself to find at least one positive thought and write it down in the table.

THE PARADOX EXERCISE AND THE MIDDLE PATH

It's time to go a step further and seek to understand the reason for your particular experience. The exercise is simple but complex (a paradox in itself!) and allows you to extract the deeper purpose of an experience.

Let's say that currently, your relationship with your partner is in danger because both of you must work enough hours in order to pay your monthly rent. You only spend one afternoon together per month, and it's not enough to sustain the relationship. You're growing apart.

Here are the opposites:

POSITIVE THOUGHTS	NEGATIVE THOUGHTS
You're earning enough money to pay the rent.	Because you're working so much, you can't provide your partner with emotional support.

To find the paradox solution, you must reconcile the opposites: 'money' must be reconciled with 'the absence of emotional support to your partner'.

The paradox: The reason you work so hard is to create a happy life for your partner, but in doing so, you're creating the opposite.

The middle path: Is there a way to create a middle path where a possible positive solution can be found? The middle path can be discovered by compromising the positive (earning money), and leveraging the negative (the absence of emotional support to your partner). The opposites fuse together and create a middle path.

Some middle path solutions: Is it possible to reduce the amount of work you do or the time you spend working – (a) perhaps by starting your own business with your partner – so you can emotionally support each other *and* make money at the same time? (b) to move to a city where rents are cheaper so that you can work less hours, or (c) if you have a spare bedroom, to sub-let it (if your contract allows) and raise the extra revenue that way?

Not only does it resolve the negative (the absence of emotional support), but it initiates a new business opportunity to achieve the positive (earning money by starting your own business). This solution has the potential to give you greater freedom in the future.

More examples could be:

EXAMPLE 2:

POSITIVE THOUGHTS	NEGATIVE THOUGHTS
You dearly love your children and you want to bring them up in a loving and harmonious environment.	You are hurting your children because of your increasingly challenging relationship with your partner.

The paradox: Through the pressures of raising children you have fallen out of love with your partner – which is negatively impacting on your children.

SOME MIDDLE PATH SOLUTIONS:

(a) could you create a childcare roster with family and friends? Thus giving you more quality time with your partner and increasing your own knowledge of how other parents raise their children.

(b) could you go for counselling with your partner and actively look for ways to improve your self-care?

(c) if you have no option but to separate, could you develop a great co-parenting relationship with your ex-partner and still have a regular family day in a neutral place together? Could this positive interaction reignite your good feeling for your ex *and* continue to reassure your children that they are supported and protected from negative outside influences?

EXAMPLE 3:

POSITIVE THOUGHTS	NEGATIVE THOUGHTS
You would like your son to make more independent decisions for himself.	Your son is being bullied at school.

The paradox: Because you gave your son permission to make more independent decisions, he has made some friendship choices that you don't agree with, and now he is being bullied at school. Currently, he needs your support more than ever.

SOME MIDDLE PATH SOLUTIONS:

(a) could you speak to your son's teacher and ask him or her to meet with your son? Maybe the teacher and your son can brainstorm different solutions together; still giving your son a sense of autonomy.

(b) could you create a coach/coachee relationship with you and your son, and ask him to resolve the problem by himself, while you stay abreast of the situation at all times? Perhaps, your son's creativity could resolve the bullying, give him more resilience as an independent problem solver, and create a less interdependent relationship between the two of you. This will require you to take a step back and trust in your son.

(c) could you speak tactfully with the parents of the child who is bullying your son, and organise a problem-solving meeting that only the two boys attend? In the meeting, your son learns how to make positive independent decisions without his parents.

THE PARADOX MEANING

Every challenge or problem that you face is infused with an extraordinary message which has the potential to make you stronger for future challenges. In the earlier example:

The husband and wife wanted to spend more time together. Now they are business partners.

Since Malala Yousafzai has founded her own non-profit organisation, she has become an adovcate for female education all over the world, giving underprivileged women the opportunity to achieve their dreams. Not only is Ms Yousafzai stronger for her future challenges with the skills she has learnt as the head of a non-profit organisation, but the women she has helped to educate are stronger as well. Here the paradox meaning for Ms Yousafzai could be:

Malala Yousafzai wanted to help underprivileged women and childen to reach their fullest potential. But it was only after she was shot and hospitalised by those who opposed her views that she was able to elevate her objectives to a world stage.

The paradox meaning is designed to enlighten the recipient of the paradox, so they can understand why they had that particular experience, and use this valuable information for future challenges. Let's take a look at another example. In chapter 1, I highlighted Nelson Mandela's Original Dream Intention: *to abolish apartheid in South Africa forever*. He wanted to overthrow apartheid but instead he was imprisoned for twenty-seven years. However, while powerless in prison he became the best-known symbol of apartheid's injustice, thereby hastening its downfall. The paradox meaning for Mr Mandela could be:

Nelson Mandela helped to overthrow apartheid by experiencing tremendous personal self-sacrifice. After years of isolation he became the country's new leader, the highest profile South African in the world.

In the following exercise, try to reconcile one of the high-priority opposites you listed in the table in exercise 10, using a middle path solution. Maybe you can find your own beautiful, personal paradox meaning, and turn your negative situation into a more positive one. Perhaps you are struggling with tragedy and loss right now and it may seem impossible to find meaning in what is happening in your life. Just hold on to your hopes, and remember, as Mr Mandela experienced, some great things take a long time to happen.

EXERCISE 11: FINDING YOUR MIDDLE PATH SOLUTION AND PARADOX MEANING

What's a middle path solution to your biggest challenge?

Can you find the paradox meaning?

INTERDEPENDENCE

If you can meet with triumph and disaster, and treat those two impostors just the same … you'll be a Man, my son!

Rudyard Kipling

When I ask people what they would like to achieve from life, the standard answer is: 'I would like to be happy.' I completely understand this goal. To finally overcome pain and suffering is a very worthwhile and honourable pursuit, but what does being happy actually mean? Does happiness mean only experiencing wonderful serene moments of peace and fulfilment?

I have already highlighted that you cannot have one opposite without the other. Two opposites that seem disconnected can actually be fused together to create a paradoxical meaning. If we follow this theory, we cannot have happiness without sadness. Therefore, in order to experience serene moments of peace and fulfilment, we must also endure moments of sorrow and grief. These two opposites are interdependent on each other. Hence, if your Dream is to achieve happiness, you must be willing and committed to experience, understand, and overcome sorrow and grief. *All* opposite qualities are interdependent on each other.

For instance, you would like to become the manager of your department at work, because you will receive more respect from your colleagues and customers, possibly have a greater sense of purpose with your career, and perhaps you may even get the corner office with the great view. All these objectives are fantastic, but what do you need to commit to, in order to accomplish it? Perhaps you must take on extra-curricular activities where you study at night after work for six months, or you must work in a company subsidiary for a year in Mexico. What pressure will you and your family experience when you work all day and then study for three hours a night, five days a week? How much will you miss your family and friends when you live in Mexico for a year? Yes, you will become manager of your department, but through what sacrifices?

We can reverse this process. Even though you will put strain on yourself with your extra studies, how much new information will you learn, how many new skills will you acquire, and how will you feel, when you become an expert in your field of expertise? Or when you live in Mexico for one year, while it will be hard on your family, you will also learn a language and develop a new network of friends/colleagues/customers that you didn't have before. This may lead to a new set of opportunities.

Can you see the interdependence of the opposities? You cannot experience happiness without its partner, sadness. They are like siamese twins, inseparable.

If you would like to find your soulmate and all the benefits that accompany having a soulmate, be prepared for moments of loneliness.

The Pursuit of Happyness is an American biographical drama starring Will Smith based on entrepreneur Chris Gardner's struggle with homelessness, and his rise to success as a stockbroker. Chris was working as a low-paid medical equipment salesman when his wife abandoned him, leaving him to pay the family's expenses. Although he had limited education and business experience, Chris applied for a training programme in a prestigious San Francisco stock brokerage firm. Only through using his ingenuity in impressing a partner at the firm in the back seat of a taxi by solving a Rubik's Cube puzzle was he offered an interview, and eventually accepted in the training programme. The programme would pay very little, but he didn't withdraw. He had a dream! He wanted to be a stockbroker, and create a financially secure life for his son and himself – something they had never had. So he began a double life.

During the day he would train, and at night he would desperately sell medical equipment – even though he and his son were now homeless. After a year of stretching himself to breaking point, Chris Gardner came first in his class and was offered a stockbroker position within the firm.

Now he is the founder & CEO of Gardner Rich & Co, a private stock brokerage firm with offices in Chicago, New York City, and San Francisco. In Chris Gardner's situation, the emotional stress of his wife abandoning the family, participating in a highly competitive training programme, and living in tremendously difficult conditions led to him becoming the founder and CEO of his own company, and creating a prosperous life for his son and himself. The facts speak for themselves. The interdependent nature of the opposites in our lives can be extremely challenging, but also incredibly powerful and life-changing.

THE OPPOSITES TREE

Let's say you have just finalised a contract for your company with a new customer. Your manager is ecstatic with your achievement, and offers you a company director position within the firm.

Is it only a positive outcome for you?

The opposites are the framework in which we live. When you are aware of the potential opposites before you enter a new situation you have the advantage of foresight to embrace the optimal decisions you can make, and avoid suffering.

Try the paradox exercise too by brainstorming and identifying middle path solutions, and thinking about the paradox meaning. This will help you to resolve any unforseeable problems.

Your new company director position

POSITIVE OUTCOMES

1. Your income increases
2. You have more authority within the company
3. You feel a greater purpose at work.

NEGATIVE OUTCOMES

1. Because you have a higher income, your expenses increase
2. You suspect colleagues are envious of your position
3. You fear losing your new status.

POSITIVE OUTCOMES

1. You buy a new home
2. You change the sales ethics of the firm
3. Your relationship with your wife improves because you are a pleasure to be around.

NEGATIVE OUTCOMES

1. You invest in high-risk company shares, and lose your money
2. Under pressure you abuse your authority, and a colleague makes a formal complaint about you
3. You become self-centred, and isolate yourself from the family.

POSITIVE OUTCOMES

1. You develop a sound financial business plan and save money
2. You give more responsibilities to your colleagues, and increase their self-confidence
3. You no longer worry about losing your position, and new opportunities arise.

NEGATIVE OUTCOMES

1. Your budget implodes, so you lose your car and house
2. You become socially isolated and depressed at work
3. The fear of losing your job creates irrational thoughts, and your work performance deteriorates.

CHAPTER SUMMARY

1. Negatives are fuelled by negative thoughts. Can you find the paradox meaning?

2. You can eventually turn a disaster into a triumph by reconciling the opposites. Can you find the paradox meaning?

3. There is always a positive – and it grows and builds momentum when you focus on and react to it. Can you find the paradox meaning?

4. In a middle path solution, the positive is compromised by looking at the situation from a different perspective in order to deal with the negative. Can you find the paradox meaning?

5. Every paradox is infused with an extraordinary meaning that makes you stronger and more aware. Can you find the paradox meaning?

6. The opposites are interdependent on each other. For example, would Chris Gardner have achieved so much without the incredible pressures he had experienced?

CALL TO ACTION

Understanding the opposites is the most effective problem-solving technique I possess. The opposites are everywhere, waiting to disclose the hidden truths of our experiences. I don't know why opposites are the framework of our existence, but I do know that if you utilise the opposites with as much vision as you can, no problem is beyond your creative capacity.

You have the power to make every experience not only positive, but an enlightened evolution into the future!

ACTION STEPS

Step 1: Make a list of all the high-priority negatives in your life, and find their opposites (see exercise 10: Reconciling opposites in your personal life).

Step 2: Now choose one situation you have listed that you feel you have the strength and creative capacity to practically achieve its middle path.

Step 3: Fuse your opposites together, create a measurable honest action plan – with dates, results, people to engage etc – and allow your extraordinary paradox meaning to evolve by itself.

Special note: Opposites are everywhere. Become a disciplined student and look for opposites in all situations with the intention of building your awareness, and therefore create a higher positive solutions success rate in your life.

CHAPTER 5

THE DOOR OF OPPORTUNITY – THE ROLE OF PERSONAL RELATIONSHIPS IN REALISING YOUR DREAM

My first keynote presentation, 'Rapport building: the key to success in sales', sought to explain the importance of relationships in sales. At the time, the Lions and Rotary clubs to which I was giving the presentation were experiencing a dramatic drop in membership enrolments. The days of club-based volunteer work for the community seemed to be fading – Generation Ys are interested in voluntary work, but tend to do it via technology.

The simple fact is, the only way the Rotary and Lions clubs can survive is through people's continual dedication to them. During the presentation, I made this point:

People are the key to your success! People stand at the door of opportunity!

Remember how my girlfriend's encouragement helped me take the plunge and begin pursuing my Dream?

We all know (I hope) the importance of relationships with others. There are 7.5 billion people in the world, and every day offers the possibility of new or continuing relationships. I'd like to focus on your proactive role in forming and nurturing personal and business relationships.

Here are some simple but complex ways (another paradox) to help other people participate positively in your Dream:

1. **Don't judge others.** It's actually very difficult to understand why other people do what they do – their icebergs are very deep because our lives are long and our experiences so complex! And someone you judge, and therefore dismiss, could be the very person who's standing at a door of opportunity for you.

2. **Help others without expectation.** Use your strengths to allow others to identify their strengths.

3. **Forgive others, even if they intentionally hurt you.** There is no greater love than forgiveness. Jesus said it best: 'Forgive them, for they do not know what they do.' People usually don't understand the full ramifications of their actions. How can you stay angry with a person who is ignorant? And if you do stay angry, then you create a 'negative/negative' situation in which nobody wins – the worst possible result!

RECONCILING OPPOSITES IN RELATIONSHIPS

Now, let's examine how 'opposites', the topic of chapter 4, apply to relationships.

It isn't a coincidence that all my past girlfriends have played integral roles in my career and my life. It's logical: if I choose a path of love and inspiration with the Dream, my journey to the Dream will teach me what it means to love another.

If you haven't already worked this out based on my Camino experience, I'm a romantic. I believe there is an ideal opposite for every person in the world – a soulmate, you could say. Current public opinion may challenge this view, and say we have several soulmates. This I certainly agree with; but, I believe we have many different types of soulmates for different life situations, and there is certainly a lifelong partner soulmate who will gradually accept all our fears and insecurities. The opposites rule in chapter 4 confirms this fact. In the ideal world your lifelong partner soulmate will be your lover, your business partner, your best friend, and share opposite qualities (whether you're in a same-sex or opposite-sex relationship).

As an example, let's look at Magdalena's versus my idea of how to recuperate after a stressful week. If it's a sunny Saturday, Magdalena's first reaction is to go outside; her recuperation technique is to move her body and enjoy the sun. My first reaction, by contrast, is to lie in bed and watch a movie. Both are successful techniques, but opposite. This leaves the two of us with a dilemma and a possible argument.

If Magdalena and I can separate ourselves from our own positions (preferring sport or movies), and can see the value of the other's opposite (so, Magdalena can see the value in watching movies and I can see the value in sport), then we can receive the full benefits of both! I'll enjoy my movies *more* after a walk in the sun, and Magdalena will enjoy her sport or walk *and* a thought-provoking movie.

If you look hard enough, you'll find endless opposites in your relationship with your partner. And if both partners compromise, both can experience the benefits of the paradox. If one of the partners doesn't compromise, this is the beginning of the deterioration process.

It will be difficult to realise the full potential of your Dream unless you are prepared to compromise and work alongside the meaningful people in your life.

EXERCISE 12: DISCOVERING YOUR SOULMATE – HOW TO FIND LIKE-MINDED PEOPLE

This exercise is both for people who've found their soulmate and people who haven't yet. It could be an exercise of confirmation between existing partners, or an exercise in discovering what qualities your soulmate might have.

In the left column of the table following, write down your skills and interests. In the right column, write down the opposite skills and interests to yours. For example: perhaps you work well with your hands; an opposite skill could be public speaking. Perhaps your interest is gardening; an opposite interest might be analysing the stock market on your computer.

I'm not going to say that your opposites or mine are completely accurate. This is a speculative exercise, but it will deepen your perception of others and allow the relationship paradox to eventuate.

But please, don't go to parties intentionally looking for your opposite! Use the exercise to increase your awareness, then let it go.

MY SKILLS AND INTERESTS	THE OPPOSITE SKILLS AND INTERESTS

Our common experiences bring us together; but paradoxically, it's our differences that ignite us.

CHAPTER SUMMARY

1. Freedom comes through being prepared to make a lifelong commitment – unless you are prepared to compromise with others, it will be difficult to realise the full potential of your Dream.

2. Our differences ignite our togetherness.

CALL TO ACTION

Through all the different stages of your life, there are people waiting to help, and be helped by you. Even though we fight, and disagree, we are in this game called life – together! You can only achieve your Dream if you have willing participants to support you.

Your soulmate needs you!

Your family, friends and colleagues need you!

The people who are vital to achieving your dreams and you theirs, whom you haven't met yet, need you!

The world is a spiderweb of relationships, and we are interdependent on each other. Please use this simple fact to embrace others without judgement. We are one big family: let's work together!

ACTION STEPS

Step 1: If you would like to develop a life-long relationship or relationships, think outside of the square. As a young man, I attended parties with the intention of finding my soulmate or a like-minded woman to share my life with. I always left disappointed. Establishing life-long relationships in either your business or your personal life depends on many different variables – which is very difficult to understand. So don't try to understand it, and focus on yourself!

Step 2: Write down a list of holidays, work situations, hobbies and experiences you would like to have.

Step 3: Prioritise your list, make your plans, and have fun! Don't be afraid to do things by yourself, and don't go looking for a partner. Make yourself the priority, and stay open to new experiences.

CHAPTER 6

THE BUSINESS COMMUNICATOR

Successful business communication is not how others relate to you, but how you adapt to them. In the previous chapter we discussed the role of personal relationships in realising your Dream. Now, I would like to focus on the other aspect of your Dream where relationships play a pivotal role in your success – business relationships.

Over thousands of years many psychologists have defined human psychology into four distinct characters:

- The four temperaments theory (Hippocrates of Kos, 460 – c. 370 BCE)
- The four psychological types (Carl Gustav Jung, 1875–1961).

For many years I have trained corporate professionals in the art of customer psychology. The basis of the theories on which I base my approach originate from William Moulton Marston's 1928 book *Emotions of Normal People*, and Inscape Publishing's contemporary DiSC personality assessment tool.

What is DiSC, and how can it allow you to effectively communicate with customers/colleagues and become a more dynamic business communicator?

Similar to earlier psychological theories, DiSC identifies four distinct personalities:

- **D**ominance
- **I**nfluence
- **S**teadiness
- **C**onscientiousness.

The DiSC model is based on two assumptions: that behaviour is circumstantial, and within those circumstances, behaviour tends to be highly consistent.

For example, if you have attended church in the past, how do people behave there? They are polite, orderly, mostly do not speak to others during the service, but perhaps they sing. Are you aware of this information before you attend church? Yes. It is a Sunday morning and you are preparing for church. During your preparations you think about what church will be like today, so you re-evaluate your church memories. Could you make a good prediction about how people will behave? Yes. Of course, your prediction will not be 100 per cent, but you can make a general forecast. Now you get out of the car with your family: what do you do? Do you enter church and behave like everybody else? Yes. Therefore, is it possible that through re-evaluating your memories you were able to adapt your behaviour to the future church service today? Yes.

Another example is a work situation with a customer. As you prepare for a meeting with a customer you've had for five years, do you analyse the past behaviour of your customer before you attend the meeting? Yes. Maybe your customer is always careful with money, or likes to do small talk for five minutes before getting into business. If they are focused on money, do you prepare your proposal to highlight how your client will save costs, or if they like small talk, do you prepare a few well-chosen topics to get the ball rolling? Yes.

This is my interpretation of the DiSC personality model:

Step 1: Evaluate behaviour of a person in a past set of circumstances

Step 2: Create the appropriate behaviours within yourself to best fit that person

Step 3: Adapt those behaviours to that person in the future situation.

I call the DiSC model 'forced empathy', because it forces you to put yourself in the other person's shoes. When you analyse the behavioural traits of a person with whom you will communicate, and then adapt your own behaviour in order to complement the other person's, you can create a strategic and efficient communication process. This process will allow you to communicate and network more effectively, accelerating the probability of success for your customer and you.

Let's take a look at the four DiSC personalities:

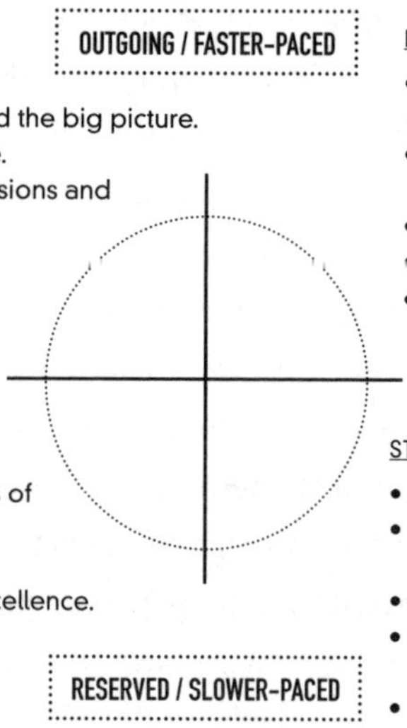

DOMINANCE

- They would like authority.
- Focused on tasks, results, and the big picture.
- They are direct and assertive.
- They like to make quick decisions and enjoy change.
- They do not like small talk.
- They are professional.

INFLUENCE

- They like to be the focal point in conversations.
- They are enthusiastic and expressive.
- They are energetic.
- They are persuasive.
- They are idealistic.

CONSCIENTIOUSNESS

- They have high expectations of themselves.
- They like details.
- They like time to achieve excellence.
- They are unsatisfied with the staus quo.
- They are relentless.

STEADINESS

- Focus on building trust with others.
- They like a calm and non-confrontational atmosphere.
- Thoughtful of other peoples' feelings.
- They enjoy a supportive and reliable environment.
- They like to work in step-by-step procedures.
- They are team orientated.

This could be the reaction of each DiSC personality when they enter an overcrowded lift:

Dominance – The dominance personality moves through the crowd to enter the lift. Once they have found their position, they wait impatiently for someone to press the button. They are not focused on engaging with others.

Influence – The influence personality sees the overcrowded lift as a socialising opportunity. They begin to tell jokes, have a laugh, and explain a very interesting story about the last time they were in an overcrowded lift.

Steadiness – The steadiness personality has their hand on the lift doors to see if anyone else is coming. Maybe there is a little bit more room for their colleagues.

Conscientiousness – The conscientiousness personality stands outside, calculating the maximum weight capacity of the lift.

I believe we have a primary and secondary personality in different work situations. Although our environment is the number one influencer of our behaviour, and every person has the capacity 'to be' any DiSC personality, depending on the situation. I call each personality:

Dominance – Dominant
Influence – The Actor
Steadiness – The Carer
Conscientiousness – The Scientist.

The four DiSC personalities could either be an obstacle or opportunity to achieve your dreams. All personalities have equally complementary qualities.

THE DIMENSIONS

In the diagram you can see the two dimensions and focuses of the personalities:

THE VERTICAL DIMENSION

Outgoing/Faster-Paced

You may have observed that colleagues in the sales department or any other high energy work environment speak quickly, love making decisions, enjoy change, and have strong opinions? These colleagues could possibly be dominance or influence personality types. From my experience, a lot of business professionals who have been promoted into managerial roles take on dominance as their primary personality, because their position demands it. They are expected to work quickly because of their increased responsibilities, and the results-focused nature of their work. Perhaps, prior to their promotion they weren't so dominant, and enjoyed a different-paced work environment.

Reserved/Slower-Paced

The conscientiousness and steadiness personalities prefer a calmer work atmosphere. They don't thrive on the rush of the moment like the dominance and influence personalities. They embrace thoughtful non-confrontational situations. These personalities can be identified through slower movements, voice and speech. For example, you regularly visit a colleague in the research and development department, and her energy is placid, but concentrated. There is no phone ringing off the hook on her desk, but she is quietly immersed in her current project. This behaviour is common with the conscientiousness personality.

THE HORIZONTAL DIMENSION

Relationships focused

The influence and steadiness personalities focus on relationships at work, although both personalities value and approach business relationships differently. For the influence personality their major motivation is to persuade and inspire others. The steadiness personality would like to support and care for others and avoid conflicts. For example, a colleague of yours is charming, quick witted, dynamic, and always has a great story to tell. During meetings she consistently engages others with her energetic body language and optimistic opinions. This behaviour is traditionally consistent with the influence personality. Another example, a customer of yours is a friendly even-tempered person, he speaks quite slowly, and is always very interested in your well being. After each meeting you feel a great bond and trust with him. This behaviour is typical of the steadiness personality.

Logic and tasks focused

The dominance and conscientiousness personalities are driven to achieve results but both personalities have different motivations and means of achieving this. The conscientiousness personality's major motivation is to achieve excellence. They are 120 per cent people. They analyse the facts and strive to improve their previous performances. Since dominance work at a fast tempo, understanding the bigger picture is more of a priority than carefully scrutinising the details. For example, your manager pays lip service to small talk. When you meet her on Monday morning, it's normally a simple hello, then down to business.

During team meetings, your manager is very professional. She is focused only on results, and becomes easily frustrated if your explanations are too long. This would constitute the dominance personality.

EXERCISE 13: YOUR DISC PERSONALITY

Please carefully analyse all the DiSC personalities and write down your primary and secondary DiSC personality at work.

Primary personality:

....

Secondary personality:

....

EXERCISE 14: IDENTIFYING YOUR COLLEAGUES' AND CUSTOMERS' DISC PERSONALITIES

Please analyse, identify and write down the DiSC personalities of your customers and colleagues. Pay special attention to those with whom your communication could be more effective.

Dominance	Influence
....	....
....	....
....	....
....	....
....	....
....	....

Conscientiousness	Steadiness
....	....
....	....
....	....
....	....
....	....
....	....

YOUR DISC COMMUNICATION TOOLBOX

The amount of opportunities you encounter in your Dream depends upon how versatile your communication is with others.

As we all noticed during our school days, there were socially popular and less popular students. There are many reasons for this, and for children and parents this phenomena can be a mystery. One possible cause is a person's lack of self-confidence and ability to engage and find common ground with others. This is a huge hindrance, because connecting with others is about asking them questions, and capturing their interest. I have observed in many international companies and in general that some people find it difficult to focus their attention on others, build empathy, and create a solid platform of common ground to ignite their working relationships.

After I left school, where I had felt like an outsider, I began working in the hospitality industry. Here I was given an opportunity to develop a skill I didn't know that I had. Since the hospitality industry is primarily face-to-face interactions with customers, I unconsciously refined my listening and questioning techniques until I unearthed a very effective communication strategy: the mirroring technique. Through trial and error, I realised effective communication can be accomplished by reflecting a person's own behaviour onto themselves. For example, if you enter a football team's locker room, I recommend you identify your masculinity as soon as possible, because there will be plenty of testosterone in the room. Once the football players identify common ground in your shared masculinities, an opportunity to build rapport will arise.

I regularly teach department managers. Most of the time, the managers are assertive, experienced, and self-confident. Therefore, in order to achieve a successful learning outcome for everyone, I need to mirror their behaviour by also being assertive, self-confident, and demonstrating my relevant experience.

To increase business opportunites and success,
we need to identify others within ourselves.

THE DISC PERSONALITIES ADAPTING AND MIRRORING STRATEGIES

DOMINANCE

- Be formal, and exhibit professionalism
- Prepare facts and results in bullet points
- Be concise and to the point
- Offer alternatives
- Give them autonomy
- Do not be submissive. Stand your ground and gain respect.

VOICE, SPEECH AND BODY MOVEMENT

- Confident, short, sharp, fast, clear, and direct.

INFLUENCE

- Prepare and ask open questions
- Listen and allow them to express themselves
- Ask for critical information in writing
- Energise yourself with enthusiasm and positivity
- Keep them on track
- Have lots of fun.

VOICE, SPEECH AND BODY MOVEMENT

- Quick expressive movements. Modulate your voice with many different tones.

CONSCIENTIOUSNESS

- Be very well prepared
- Concentrate on quality and details
- Be consistent with your facts and figures
- Double-check your research comes from reilable sources
- Explain the end goals, and big picture
- Set accountable time frames.

VOICE, SPEECH AND BODY MOVEMENT

- Purposeful and slow

STEADINESS

- Build empathy and trust
- Avoid confrontation and conflict
- Support, reassure, and care
- Create step-by-step processes and counsel through change
- Focus on teamwork.

VOICE, SPEECH AND BODY MOVEMENT

- Soft, slow and gentle.

SOME EXAMPLES:

DEALING WITH DOMINANCE

Situation:

You are an engineer at an IT company, and your customer has invited you to a problem-solving meeting because the current IT system has been malfunctioning. They sent you a short, direct email, and demanded your participation in a meeting tomorrow.

Possible adapting and mirroring strategy:

You've had many meetings with this customer in the past, and you have observed that the customer enjoys being the authority and making the decisions. You carefully prepare questions for the meeting that allow the customer to make the final decision. Also, you prepare a bullet-point document that only focuses on the facts and results. Because your customer always speaks quickly and to the point, you memorise your key points so you can deliver the information quickly. You also wear your best suit.

DEALING WITH INFLUENCE

Situation:

You have been promoted to the head of the sales department in your company. Your first project is to secure a contract with a leading software supplier. You have organised a meeting with Mr Jones, the head of the purchasing department, to introduce your product, and establish a relationship. Your colleague has informed you that Mr Jones appreciates small talk and being the centre of attention.

Possible adapting and mirroring strategy:

You canvas colleagues to discover Mr Jones' hobbies, likes/dislikes, and you prepare thoughtful questions that will allow Mr Jones to be the focal point of the conversation. You organise to meet at a restaurant, and not his office, because you would like to create a relaxed atmosphere. You design your presentation in a creative way and memorise the key points so you can deliver the information quickly. You wear bright clothes, and you aim to be optimistic and have fun.

DEALING WITH STEADINESS

Situation:

You are a team leader, and your manager has asked you to collect vital information for her powerpoint presentation tomorrow morning. She has instructed you that the necessary information is available inhouse but your deadline to collect all information is 5pm today! You are under pressure. It is now 8am, and you have identified Sandra as the responsible person. When you organise the meeting, Sandra informs you that two of her colleagues have called in sick, she is overwhelmed with work, and can't possibly provide the information you requested by the end of the day.

Possible adapting and mirroring strategy:

It is clear that Sandra is also under pressure, but you need those documents for your manager. You prepare a supportive step-by-step process that Sandra can easily follow to obtain the information you need. You also develop some ideas to relieve Sandra's workload. When you arrive at the meeting you create a calm, non-threatening atmosphere. Your voice is slow, soft and reassuring. You stay open, listen and care for Sandra's situation. You then introduce your step-by-step process.

DEALING WITH CONSCIENTIOUSNESS

Situation:

You are a project manager in an electrical parts company. Your customer has requested a statistical performance summary analysis of a particular product. The customer has reiterated that only a general summary is necessary. Your deadline is two days away. John, your colleague, works in the quality management department and is responsible for this information. You have a good business relationship with John, but you are aware that he always misses deadlines because of his perfectionism.

Possible adapting and mirroring strategy:
Since John is a perfectionist, you have decided to provide him with all available details for the statistical performance summary analysis, plus you create an indepth breakdown of the customer's request. You give John more time than is necessary to complete the analysis, but you organise consistent updates to review his progress.

EXERCISE 15: DISC IMPLEMENTATION PLAN

Pinpoint a regular situation where you encounter each DiSC personality and consider how your interaction could be substantially improved by creating possible adapting and mirroring strategies.

DOMINANCE

INFLUENCE

STEADINESS

CONSCIENTIOUSNESS

CHAPTER SUMMARY

1. Thoughtfully preparing your communication with the four DiSC personalities will help to accelerate your dreams.

2. Remember to be versatile with your communication.

3. Freedom comes with a price tag, and in order to increase business opportunites and success we need to identify others within ourselves.

4. Empathy is taking the time to understand others.

CALL TO ACTION

I am always discouraged when I observe extremely talented and intelligent business professionals who are unable to adapt their communication skills to accommodate others. What is the point of having a fast car when you drive it at 50 mph?

All businesses in all industries around the world rely on their employees' ability to competently communicate with their customers and colleagues. The most profitable communication strategy is 'forced empathy' – recognising, analysing, adapting, and mirroring the DiSC personalities. Let go of your time schedule, and show genuine interest in your customers. They may not notice your communication technique, but they will appreciate the common ground and shared values you have established.

ACTION STEPS

Step 1: Make a list of customers and colleagues with whom you feel you could improve your relationship. Also, make a list of customers and colleagues whom you would like to have a business relationship with in the future.

Step 2: Identify the DiSC personality for each person. Please keep in mind not only the adapting and mirroring behaviours in the table, but also the DiSC personality's movement, voice and speech tempo.

Step 3: Create step-by-step measurable action plans and evaluate your own progress.

CHAPTER 7

HELPING OTHERS – THE THREE LAWS OF NETWORKING

Helping others is where your Dream:

- derives its motivation and energy
- gets its momentum, and
- discovers its eventual outcome – within yourself.

If your Original Dream Intention doesn't currently incorporate positively influencing or helping other people, then please reword it so it does. My Original Dream Intention was 'to positively change the realities of others'. 'Others' are the object of my actions, and without them, my Dream can't exist. That's how important helping others is to your Dream and the world!

The information in this chapter has been a personal life lesson for me, and is still an ongoing process. First, let's look at helping others from the business point of view.

BUSINESS NETWORKING AND CREATING OPPORTUNITIES

I tend to use the word 'karma' when I talk about helping others, but it's not a widely accepted term within the business environment. So in this chapter I'll use the term 'networking' instead. A good 'networking' definition is:

A chance to meet people; learn; swap ideas, stories and contacts; and potentially create mutually beneficial opportunities.

Based on my research, networking accounts for up to eighty-seven per cent of business in the marketplace.

There are three universal laws that form the foundations of ethical networking:

1. The Law of Reciprocity
2. The Law of Abundance
3. The Law of Giving Without Expectation.

1. THE LAW OF RECIPROCITY

In essence, the Law of Reciprocity is:

What you give out comes back tenfold, but not always from the same person.

As I said earlier, it's important to create a positive networking environment by giving without expectation and not letting money get in the way of the Dream. Monetary gain is only one marker of success.

Wayne Bennett asks: 'Which wolf are you feeding?'. If you are focusing on a short-term remuneration – which is fine – what will you receive? Another short-term remuneration! What comes next? Another short-term remuneration?! And so forth.

Giving without expectation is greater than money: in fact, it's a currency in itself. 'What you give to others comes back tenfold.' This simple but complex (and paradoxical) law of networking is the engine of your future business and personal success.

I've mentioned that I gave over fifty *free* keynote presentations to Rotary and Lions. What did I receive in return? My first corporate facilitator opportunity, worth AU$60,000 per annum. Let's do the maths of the first networking law in this situation. These are not exact figures, of course, but they prove a point.

Personal costs (money and time)	
Fifty free keynote presentations to Rotary and Lions clubs. Per keynote presentation, in Australian dollars:	
Travel:	$30 in petrol (that's generous)
Car repairs, etc:	$30
Clothing costs (dry cleaning, etc):	$2
Telephone calls:	$5
Time:	5 hours (including preparation)
Sales and advertising (including website, company brochure, business card design and maintenance):	
Cost:	$15
Time:	2 hours
Total cost:	**$82**
Total time:	**7 hours**

Now, let's compare the costs of the Law of Reciprocity with the outcome, a soft-skills facilitator position:

Free keynote presentations to Rotary and Lions clubs		**Corporate soft-skills facilitator position**	
Total costs per presentation: Total time per presentation: Total costs per 50 presentations: Total time per 50 presentations:	$82 7 hours $4,100 350 hours	Salary per annum: Total time costs:	AU$60,000 It's my career.

The keynote presentations were given over two years, so the Law of Reciprocity has given me a profit per year of:

- AU$57,950, and
- 175 hours compared to a lifetime career.

I don't think a Wall Street stockbroker could offer that profit margin without doing something illegal! And we could also show the value that those fifty free keynote presentations provided to others. On average, each presentation had fifteen people in the audience, so 750 people received valuable information which possibly changed their lives or the lives of others.

The facts speak for themselves. The first networking law, the Law of Reciprocity, is a life-changer. If you give without seeking to receive something of value in return, what you may receive is beyond your imagination. So please don't allow money and security to be the sole motivators for your career choices and your Dream. The Law of Reciprocity means there's a whole different game that you can play, with unbelievable rewards.

I haven't even included the priceless benefits for myself in this example. What did I gain from my fifty free keynote presentations, on a personal level? Improved self-esteem, confidence, fulfilment, success, enjoyment, gratitude – the list could go on and on. Everyone has heard of 'win/win' situations at work: well, the Law of Reciprocity creates 'win/win/win' situations.

When you give someone something of value for free, a ripple effect begins. For example, my presentation increased my chances of career success (win), it increased the Rotary and Lions club members' chances of career and personal success (win), *and* if any club members who participated in the keynote presentation informed others of the presentation content or my services, then a third party benefitted (win). You can see how this works. Then a fourth party or fifth party could benefit, and so it goes on. It's a limitless process of unconditional giving which profits everyone who's directly or indirectly connected to it.

Giving is a natural part of life.

We naturally give to family, friends, colleagues and strangers without expectation. If an old lady falls to the ground as you're walking down the street, your natural reaction (I hope) is to offer assistance. You don't ask for anything in return. If you want to realise the full capacity of your Dream, then aim high and give with abundance. Don't think small, think BIG! Let yourself go! You'll receive abundance if you give with abundance.

If you choose a small act of giving, that's the 'frequency level' you'll enter and receive in return. But if you go big with your giving, your Dream will enter that level too.

EXERCISE 16: THE LAW OF RECIPROCITY

Review your actions over the last week. What, when, where and to whom did you give freely?

What, when, where and to whom could you possibly offer something for free in the future? Please think big!

The 'Outcome, Purpose, Action' (OPA) identifies measurable outcomes or objectives. It's designed to clarify each individual step of your action plan to realise your goal.

What's your OPA with your free acts of giving?

Outcome	What do you want? Be specific. How will you know you've achieved this outcome?	
Purpose	Why do you want it? What will it give you? How will you feel?	
Action	What are the steps? Which free actions do you need to take? When will you do it? How long will it take you to achieve it?	1. 2. 3. 4.

I'm planning to give thirty copies of this book, *The Dream*, away for free to my family, friends and colleagues. I don't know what will come about from this act of giving – but I know that if I do it without expectation, the ripple effect will begin.

2. THE LAW OF ABUNDANCE

'To live a pure, unselfish life, one must count nothing as one's own in the midst of abundance.'

Buddha

Put simply, the Law of Abundance is:

There is plenty for everyone – opportunities on a local, national or international level.

The second law of networking, the Law of Abundance, cannot exist unless the first law of networking, the Law of Reciprocity, is in play. Author Darryl Anka calls it 'the frequency of reality':

Everything is energy and that's all there is to it. Match the frequency of the reality you want and you cannot help but get that reality. It can be no other way. This is not philosophy. This is physics.

The only way you enter the frequency level of a certain reality is through the act of giving. The Law of Abundance is a reactionary law. It gives abundance within the framework of the first networking law, the Law of Reciprocity.

Only through personal commitment and sacrifice can you realise a 'wonderful' frequency of reality.

Now, go back to your OPA table in the Law of Reciprocity section and review your outcome. How much are you committing to your free acts of giving? If it's too little, increase it! Are you going to help your children with their homework, or are you going to help ten non-profit organisations and positively influence thousands of people? The choice is yours – 'To infinity and beyond' as Buzz Lightyear said. (My friends and I repeated this quote every morning on the Camino before beginning the day's walk.)

And remember: what you receive from your selfless acts of giving may come from an unexpected source.

3. THE LAW OF GIVING WITHOUT EXPECTATION

'Good networkers give without remembering and receive without forgetting.'

Ivan Misner, *Masters of Networking*

Basically, the third and last law of networking is:

Help others without the expectation of receiving something in return.

If you give with expectation, then the first two networking laws will not apply.

This is the law that I have found most difficult. Earlier, I mentioned that I'd expected to become a movie star because of the effort I'd put into my acting studies. This expectation resulted in more than a year of depression and subconscious self-destruction.

Giving with expectation is dangerous – and in fact, you aren't actually giving if you expect something in return. I know as humans we're mainly focused on self-interested pursuits, except with our children. But if you can take yourself out of the equation, what's left?

EXERCISE 17: WHAT'S YOUR MOTIVE?

Again, go back to your OPA table earlier in the chapter. Do you have a subconscious or conscious expectation or motive? Why are you really giving?

A good motive or intention for giving might be, 'To have a more fulfilling work life that allows others and myself to reach our full potential.' Even though 'I' is part of the intention, it isn't the primary objective. The key word here is 'others.'

By contrast, a faulty motive or intention for giving would be, 'I'd like to have more money and buy the house I've always dreamt of.' Here, money and shelter are the primary source of your intention. There's nothing wrong with money and a house as indirect results, but if they're your main motive, what and how much must you suffer in order to achieve your objectives?

Do you remember that I'd asked life to match me with a woman who would help me in my career? That's an example of a faulty intention which caused me to suffer – my relationship with Joanne and subsequent role at her company impacted on my health. Yes, I wanted to move forward with my career, but at what cost?

Save yourself a lot of suffering by being wise with your intention and giving without expectation. Choose an objective that will benefit others first, and that helps you as a by-product.

When I was a young man, I read this story by Elizabeth Silance Ballard about a primary school teacher and her student.

Mrs Thompson taught a young boy called Teddy Stoddard. Mrs Thompson was consistently disappointed with Teddy's results and his inability to socialise with his peers. She found it necessary to give him Fs. During the year, Mrs Thompson was responsible for reviewing each student's past records. When she reviewed Teddy's she was immediately startled! Teddy's old teachers wrote admirably about Teddy's attitude and results, highlighting his ability to build rapport with other students. Until one teacher commented: 'The death of Teddy's mother, and lack of support from his father will continue to have a negative effect on Teddy's school results.' Mrs Thompson almost fell off her chair. She instantly identified Teddy's problem, and she felt complete regret for her behaviour.

Over the next six months Mrs Thompson gave Teddy her complete attention without any expectations. At the end of the year, and for many years after, Teddy wrote to Mrs Thompson that she was his best teacher ever. Ten years later Teddy signed his letter to Mrs Thompson with: Theodore F. Stoddard, M.D.

When Mrs Thompson decided to help Teddy, and her primary objective was to create benefit without any expectation, Mrs Thompson and Teddy Stoddard entered a completely different frequency of reality. A frequency of reality that saved Teddy's life, and made Mrs Thompson a better teacher for her future students.

EXERCISE 18: SETTING THE INTENTION FOR YOUR GIVING

Write down exactly what you intend to achieve from your free act of giving. Be descriptive, but be careful with your words.

GIVING WITHOUT EXPECTATION IN A PERSONAL SITUATION

Giving without expectation to family, friends and close colleagues can be very challenging. The people we love can hurt us the most (another paradox!), because of our investment in the person and situation we share. If you let people into your heart, they could well poison you – but if you don't let them in, you'll never know what love is. It's yet another paradox, one that's the subject of many movies and songs.

When I returned to Sydney for a visit after two years abroad, I was faced with a harsh truth: nobody really understands how I feel! I remember thinking, as I flew back, that my family and friends were going to congratulate me for my achievements in integrating into Germany, learning a new language and starting my own business. I imagined moments of celebration with them.

When I arrived home, though, the opposite occurred. Some of my family and friends didn't show any interest at all in my life in Germany – they were too preoccupied with their own lives. My frustration increased, and I finally revealed my subconscious expectation to two close friends: 'Why don't people care? Don't they know what I've been through?'

As I heard myself say the words, I realised that my lifelong tendency to give with expectation had shown its ugly face again. I *expected* people to be interested and to understand what I'd achieved in Germany, setting myself up for frustration and suffering. Not a good result! We can *hope* people will be interested, but we can't expect them to be, because other people's lives can be as full as our own.

Two years later when I returned to Australia again, I was smarter. My only intention was to look my family and friends in the eyes, to listen and to love them – a free act of giving. I didn't include myself in the objective at all. And I was free! My whole stay was full of peace, love and unexpected, happy events. I felt an honest connection with my family and friends, and I was even given wonderful direct and indirect acknowledgements of my achievements in Germany. This time I didn't expect it, but I received it anyway. Another paradox.

Have goals for your personal relationships
but don't expect anything in return from people,
especially the ones you love.

The motivations of people's behaviour are often a mystery. For example you have a colleague at work who isn't maintaining his responsibilities, and this is haemorrhaging into your client results. You are frustrated and upset with your colleague. So you take him aside and confront him on this issue. Your colleague admits and apologises for his lack of productivity, but he also explains that his mother was recently diagnosed with a terminal illness, and her treatment takes up all his time. Suddenly, you feel embarrassed by your behaviour.

People have their own agendas and issues. As we discussed in the chapter on Vipassana, a person's behaviour is the result of a very complex process. Don't judge others for their shortcomings; they're doing the best they can in the circumstances they've been given. Once you understand this, you can break free from the 'vicious expectation cycle' and nobody can hurt you.

Great lessons about expectation can be learnt from the people you love; this too is part of the Dream.

CHAPTER SUMMARY

1. Giving is a natural part of life.

2. If you give little, you'll receive little; if you give much, you'll receive much.

3. A 'wonderful' frequency of reality can only be achieved with commitment and sacrifice.

4. The return from your giving may come from an unexpected source.

EXERCISE 19: AN UNEXPECTED SOURCE

Take a moment and analyse past situations: what, where, why, and to whom did you give without expectations, but received a return from your giving from an unexpected source? What surprises will you find?

5. You can have goals for your relationships, but lower your expectations of other people.

CALL TO ACTION

The art of networking is simply art! You can leverage the interconnectedness of life to your advantage, by helping others. Either through a business or personal pursuit, if you give because you *want* to give, without expecting anything in return, then the world is yours, and everything it embodies.

Completely give yourself responsibly to the well-being of others, and you will become the master artist of your life.

ACTION STEPS

Step 1: Review the parts of your life that need a facelift, or a new and innovative idea. What needs to be energised and given new life?

Step 2: Return to exercise 16 (the Law of Reciprocity), and begin planning.

Step 3: Now, go for it! Remember the three networking laws and make your goals a reality.

CHAPTER 8

A JOURNEY OF PERSONAL DEVELOPMENT

Taking time off from your everyday life to pursue a journey of personal growth can provide you with valuable perspective and even fast-track your career. For many business professionals, only having twenty-eight annual leave days per year can limit a person's creativity. Sometimes a fresh perspective in a new environment can develop and catapult new thoughts and actions, consequently creating new opportunities and fast-tracking your career. A journey of personal development can also positively affect your entire Dream, not just its career aspect. A journey outside of your comfort zone can change your life forever, as it did mine.

You may be between jobs or you may be a freelancer able to choose when to take a longer break. If you are restricted by the amount of annual and unpaid leave you can take, a shorter journey can still represent a genuine change from your usual routine and may work wonders for revitalising your perspective on life.

> Your journey for inward development could involve anything, anywhere.

It could be finally doing that community service work you always wanted to do. It could be working for Global Camps in Africa helping to provide AIDS awareness. It could be climbing a mountain in the Himalayas. I don't know what's in store for you.

In 2010, I decided to walk the Camino de Santiago, the Way of St James. The catalyst for this decision was reading *The Pilgrimage* by Paulo Coelho, which highlighted one man's struggle and determination to discover the secrets of life on a pilgrimage. I decided to investigate whether the pilgrimage in the book existed. To my surprise, it did, and people walked it every year! I read John Brierley's book *A Pilgrim's Guide to the Camino de Santiago*, and after several months of research and preparation, including negotiations with my employer, my bags were packed.

The Dream will find the right time for you to embark on a journey of inward development. Be sure to accept the invitation when it arrives!

The first time I entered Europe was through the gates of Paris. I was a thirty-two-year-old man, but walking through the City of Light's overwhelmingly beautiful and intimidating streets, I felt like a young boy. I didn't spend long in Paris, however, quickly making my way to Saint-Jean-Pied-de-Port, the beginning of my pilgrimage.

PEOPLE ARE THE KEY

From the moment I set foot on the Camino, I found instant friends in my fellow pilgrims. That is the Camino. All you have is the bag on your back, your feet, and the relationships you share with others. Empathy levels are higher between pilgrims than in normal nine-to-five life, so it's easier to engage in conversations and create connections. It really has been the best holiday of my life so far.

People are the key to growth: so choose a journey that will allow you to interact with people like never before, even if the thought fills you with apprehension. If you are naturally reserved, you should also choose an interactive journey with others, but be aware of your limitations. Challenge yourself, but too much pressure is counter-productive.

After two weeks of walking, and developing many fulfilling connections, I found myself alone for a while – it was just the Camino and I. One day, I got lost and wandered off the traditional path onto the French way. (The Camino has many different routes or 'ways' through Spain and Europe.) That afternoon I arrived at an *albergue* (pilgrim hostel) and settled in for the night. I was chatting with fellow pilgrims before dinner when two young ladies came in, wearing almost identical clothing. I later found out that those clothes, in particular their t-shirts, were a departing gift to celebrate their trip together.

I judged them to be fresh to the Camino, so I took it upon myself to invite them to dinner and give them some friendly tips for their travels ahead. I found out that their names were Alexandra and Magdalena and that they were from Bavaria, Germany. They accepted the dinner invitation, but for some reason didn't seem to welcome my priceless advice! The following morning I didn't see them and I continued on the Camino solo.

Judgement restricts your ability to communicate and makes opportunities to connect less likely to arise.

A day later, I'd just finished my breakfast and begun to walk when the same two uninterested young women from the *albergue* caught my attention. They were picking flowers and laughing together.

Should I approach them? I wondered. Our last interaction wasn't that positive.

After a few moments, I decided to say hello.

Try to stay open to all experiences, no matter how much baggage you're carrying. You never know who could be the exact person you need, or who needs you.

EXERCISE 20: SOMEONE UNEXPECTED

Please think of two or three situations where you have helped someone you didn't set out to, or you've been helped by someone unexpected.

What were the results from your or their acts of kindness?

Have you ever had an experience with a person or people that began negatively, but had a positive outcome?

Our common experiences bring us together, but paradoxically, it's our differences that ignite us.

When I introduced myself to them again I received a lukewarm welcome, because of my 'Mr Know It All' behaviour during our first meeting, but after a few minutes of small talk we started walking together. Thirty minutes later, we were engaged in friendly banter. Over the next two weeks, the three of us became as thick as thieves. We didn't leave each other's sides, walking together through heat, wind and a day of heavy rain. And Magdalena and I realised we were attracted to each other.

The problem was, she was out of bounds: Magdalena had a boyfriend. Off limits! I'd stepped on another man's turf before, and had made the decision never to do it again, in the spirit of treating others as I would like to be treated. After two weeks, tension was running high between us, and I felt the honourable choice was to leave, so I repressed my feelings and said goodbye.

Two days later, I reunited with some pilgrim friends I had met earlier on the way. Magdalena was at the forefront of my mind, but I had to move on.

Life will never be yours until you let unhealthy attachments go. We *all* hold on to things, especially the things we love. The paradox is, holding onto something too tightly can hinder its potential, thus creating the opposite outcome to your original loving intention.

A HEALTHY ATTACHMENT

You would like to jog three times a week. It is important to your health and life balance, plus you enjoy the fresh air. Sometimes work or personal responsibilities take priority, and you may only run once or twice a week, perhaps not at all. This is ok, but you are still committed to jogging, and when the opportunity appears you will continue your hobby.

AN UNHEALTHY ATTACHMENT

You jog three times a week, because it is vital to sustain your health. Even though your work or personal responsibilities have increased, you 'must' maintain your sport routine, even if it means running at 9pm before bed.

As you can see there is a vast difference between the two attachments. The healthy attachment has positive intentions, but doesn't make you feel under the cosh. It is a personal commitment with flexibility. On the other hand, the unhealthy attachment *does* make you feel under pressure. There is no negotiating with this attachment; therefore, it achieves the opposite result, and creates more stress in your life, because you feel you have to do it.

Even so, the healthy attachment could become lackadaisical, and you may look for reasons not to jog. Then the healthy attachment has a negative result. Finding a balance between commitment and flexibility is the healthiest choice.

THE END OF THE WALK – BUT NOT THE JOURNEY

I was only a few days away from Santiago and the end of my pilgrimage. After a month of walking, I couldn't wait to arrive.

It was late afternoon and I was drinking in a bar with fellow pilgrims when my phone rang. It was Ricardo, a Mexican friend I had met on the Camino, and I left the bar so I could hear him properly. As I was walking down an alley in the middle of nowhere, who did I meet walking in the other direction? Alexandra and Magdalena! All three of us were surprised by this unexpected rendezvous; I invited them for a drink. At the end of the night it was clear that the attraction between Magdalena and I was as powerful as ever, but my mind was made up: I had to stay strong. The next day, I continued my walk without them.

My friends and I arrived in Santiago, the end of the Camino, at six o'clock in the morning. We'd come up with the brilliant idea of getting up at 2am and walking into the city at sunrise, but unfortunately it was an overcast day and we saw no sunrise. Regardless, once we received our

Camino completion certificates and settled into our accommodation, we began to *party*! We'd done it! Eight hundred kilometres at twenty-five kilometres a day for four and a half weeks – no blisters and no buses!

The next day in the late afternoon, I was walking through the city – and who did I meet? You guessed it: Alexandra and Magdalena again. We exchanged pleasantries.

EXPECT THE UNEXPECTED!

I spent the last night in Santiago at a bar. Two close friends and I had already decided to continue our pilgrimage to Cape Finisterre, the Romans' 'end of the world', the following day and truly finish the Camino. It was only another three days of walking.

Emotions were running high: the Camino is such a personal yet unifying experience, and people become very close to each other. An American friend and I were sitting at the bar watching our friends laugh, talk, hug, cry and get pretty 'friendly' with each other. As we sat there, I realised that I regretted letting the opportunities with Magdalena slip through my fingers. I regretted not embracing the natural instinct that was drawing us together, even though the circumstances made me question it. In a plea for redemption, I promised the gods, 'If I see Magdalena again, I won't let her go.'

The gods heard my prayer: ten minutes later, Magdalena walked past the front window of the bar with Alexandra. I jumped out of my seat, ran to her, and told her plainly, 'We need to go for a walk.'

The next few hours were intoxicating. At one stage, I pulled Magdalena into my arms and kissed her. I'd broken my rule, but it felt right. Magdalena was totally surprised, however, and couldn't understand why I'd suddenly changed my mind. She was leaving in the morning, and was also torn between her feelings for her boyfriend, and an uncertain future with me.

You can swim with life's current or fight against it, but either way the current will flow on.

I tried my utmost to persuade her to come to Cape Finisterre with us, but her flight back to Germany was booked and she had to return. As we said our goodbyes, we made a promise to each other: 'The first person to make contact and initiate the next step …'

The next three days held a sense of victory, but also anxious wonder. Each day our glimpse of the ocean – the magical blue ocean – became a little bigger. It seduced me. At the same time, my Camino experiences with Magdalena were on repeat in my head. What do I do now? I thought. I hope I haven't lost her email address! Are we going to see each other again?

We arrived in Cape Finisterre early in the morning, and met a German who invited us to stay at his campsite. He was a very interesting person, a former businessman who had decided to leave the capitalist world to find solace and peace living off the land. But I had other things on my mind. Magdalena! I had to email her.

The next day I found an internet café and made up my mind: I was going to Germany to see her. I wrote her an email saying so and got a positive response, and within three days I was on my way to Munich, where Magdalena and I spent two of the most romantic weeks we have ever experienced. We fell in love.

At the end of those two weeks, we exchanged stones of loyalty and committed to each other in Munich's English Garden. Three months later, I came back to Munich to begin our life together. And after five memorable years, we married and pledged our lives to one another.

And it all happened as a result of following my Original Dream Intention! I had wanted to positively change people's realities, and in order to do that, I needed to reboot on a journey of personal development. The Dream had new plans for me, but at the time I was unaware of them. In retrospect, I needed the Camino to advance the development of my Original Dream Intention.

THE DREAM IS LIMITLESS.

If you're feeling disillusioned with your current situation, whether in the work or personal spheres, please don't be afraid to rock the boat and allow the world to be your oyster. Step out with courage and determination and commit to a new experience that could change your life forever!

YOUR JOURNEY

You need to be ready and open to the journey's invitation when it comes. If you want to do some preparation and set the process in motion, then I recommend you begin investigating your options using the following exercise. Once you've invested enough thought and energy into it, your journey will unfold when you least expect it. Embrace it with everything you have!

EXERCISE 21: EXPLORING JOURNEY OPTIONS

A journey you take for personal growth should meet three criteria – it should involve a new activity, a new place and a new challenge. It's imperative to choose something that you'd dearly love to do, because love, and the magnificent motivation that accompanies it, is ideally connected to your Original Dream Intention. And if you choose a situation that's completely new, there's a greater potential for growth.

Write down a few ideas in each of these areas:

- Something you've never done before

- A place you've never been before (this doesn't have to be abroad)

- A challenge you're not sure you can accomplish, but would really like to try

As I said earlier, people are the key to growth. What kind of journey will allow you to interact with others in a way you've never done before?

Lastly, think about how long you'd like your journey to go for. I recommend giving yourself at least a few months (minimum six weeks) to immerse yourself in the experience if that is possible for you. If it's not, you could see if it's possible to use bank holidays or unpaid leave to extend your annual leave.

CHAPTER SUMMARY

1. Your journey will happen at the right time for you, although it may not seem so at the time – just be sure to accept the invitation. Your future is based on many different variables – your and other people's intentions can dramatically change. Originally I had planned to do the Camino in 2008, until my circumstances postponed the journey.

2. Our interactions with people are the key to growth, so choose a journey that will allow you to interact with others.

3. Judging other people restricts your opportunities and ability to communicate.

4. Stay open to all experiences: you never know who could be the exact person you need or vice versa.

5. Life will not be truly yours until you let go of unhealthy attachments that you have outgrown.

6. Expect the unexpected.

7. You can either swim with life's current or fight against it, but you can't stop it.

8. The Dream is limitless.

9. The possible journeys for inward development are endless.

CALL TO ACTION

How do you truly understand your local community without comparing it to another? You can't. Holidays are necessary to rejuvenate your energy for the next working cycle, but a journey of personal development will rejuvenate your life. Take a sabbatical that won't only give you much needed relaxation time, but will develop your life perspective, and create new opportunities, both at home and abroad. Step outside of your comfort zone, while simultaneously reflecting on your current life situation. Who knows what or who you will discover?

ACTION STEPS

Step 1: Please write down a list of sabbaticals you have always dreamt of taking.

Step 2: Carefully analyse each sabbatical:

- What is your inspiration behind each of these sabbaticals?
- Which ones are jumping off the page, and are calling you? Prioritise your top three.
- Carefully investigate the viability of your top three sabbaticals with your personal and work responsibilities, and budget.

Step 3: While negotiating the research process, one sabbatical will become the clear choice. Now make it a reality! Thoroughly plan your journey with the resources you have available. And remember: your journey will happen at the right time for you. Do not be disappointed when life forces you to postpone your chosen sabbatical, or gives you a different option which originally you didn't plan for. Be patient, but determined to fulfil the journey of your dreams!

Celebrating my thirty-second birthday on the Camino de Santiago, May 2010

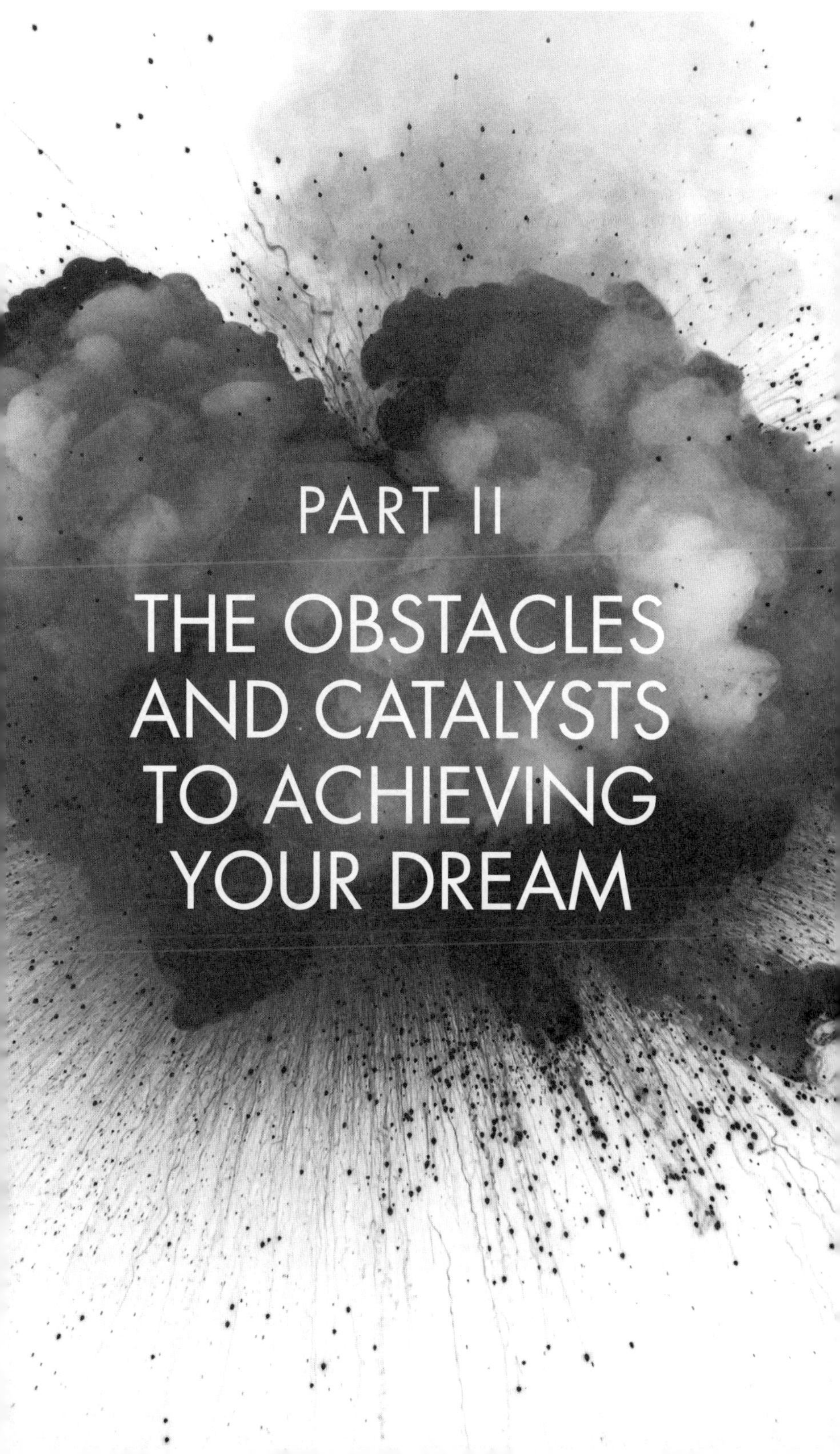

PART II

THE OBSTACLES AND CATALYSTS TO ACHIEVING YOUR DREAM

CHAPTER 9

THE FIVE DARK KNIGHTS OF THE SUFFERING MIND

So far in this book, I've shown you ways you can achieve your life's fullest potential through your Dream. But I'd be irresponsible not to also disclose the ways you can be prevented from achieving the Dream. So let's go ahead and discuss how your own mind purposefully sabotages you in following your dreams.

This chapter explores the Buddhist concept of suffering and how to avoid it. Why Buddhism? Because, in my long search for answers, I've found Buddhism's 'Four Noble Truths' to offer the best description of life and how it works. I hope they resonate with you as well.

THE TRUTH ABOUT SUFFERING

The Four Noble Truths are:

1. The truth of what suffering is (*dukkha*)
2. The truth about the causes of suffering (*samudāya*)
3. The truth that suffering can be ended (*nirodha*)
4. The truth to the path that frees us from suffering (*magga*).

I will be focusing on the first two Noble Truths, *dukkha* and *samudāya*.

Dukkha explains that we are born into suffering. When we're born, our first reaction is to cry for our mother's milk. Let's not mince words: we're suffering! Ask any parent of a three-month-old child: the child suffers most days because of its need for milk to survive. Now, I don't mean to paint a gloomy picture of life. Life is wonderful! However, the first Noble Truth shows us that we live in an impermanent, conditional and changing world which can materialise into pain.

Samudāya, the second Noble Truth, explains why suffering exists – because we have thirsts and cravings (like the baby's thirst for its mother's milk), and these exist in a temporary, conditional, changing world. In other words, your cravings can never be fully satisfied, because both the cravings and the satisfaction are temporary. They will end! So having your needs met can't give you everlasting contentment. This means that even the greatest of pleasures (like orgasms or eating particularly delicious food) can be the catalysts of suffering. We know that the experiences don't last forever, as we continue to seek fulfilment in them. We become slaves to them. Have you heard the saying, 'The definition of insanity is repeating the same action and expecting a different result'?

Our minds continue to seek lasting happiness in external gratifications, no matter how many times this approach fails.

In order to realise our Dreams, we must create defence mechanisms against our thirsts and cravings.

The only way this can be done is through the practice of Vipassana (see chapter 3) and Buddhism's 'Eightfold Path'. The modern interpretation of the Eightfold Path that I recommend is illustrated below.

The Eightfold Path of Buddhism

The Eightfold Path is the subject of many books in itself, but I won't go into details about it here. I would recommend, though, that you do your own research into it, as it's the best tool I've found to overcome the suffering mind in order to actualise the Dream.

The Eightfold Path is the fourth Noble Truth – the truth to the path that frees us from suffering (*magga*). It advises us to:

- Be aware that our actions have consequences
- Be compassionate towards others
- Use our words responsibly

- Don't intentionally hurt others
- Only consume what we need – food and other material things etc
- Protect ourselves from corrupting feelings of desire
- Be mindful: always know why we make a decision
- Meditate (see chapter 3: Vipassana).

What I want to focus on are the causes of these cravings, because if we understand the opposites (suffering versus not suffering) the paradox can materialise and awaken the Dream.

THE FIVE DARK KNIGHTS

I received some instruction from a Sri Lankan Buddhist monk, whose teaching has had a huge impact on my life and my self-awareness. In some of our discussions, he told me of five basic 'concentrations' of the mind. I call these the 'Five Dark Knights', and my interpretations of these 'concentrations' are:

1. Laziness
2. Endless searching
3. Doubt
4. Blame
5. Desire.

The Knights can work both individually and as a connected network. They're powerful, and when they work together they can bring most people to their knees. Here's a venn diagram showing how I see the Five Dark Knights network:

The interaction of the Five Dark Knights

The fact of the matter is that we need the Dark Knights in order to fulfil our dreams. They're the primary catalysts of fulfilment because they test our belief, dedication and trust. It sounds strange, but it's true. The real question is: will you allow the Dark Knights to set you free, or break you?

The best form of defence against the Dark Knights is to not react to them. When you don't react to their torturous thoughts, you give them no impetus to grow. Only by observing and mindfully acknowledging these thoughts, but not reacting to them and surrendering to the moment, can you materialise your Dream. If the Dark Knights are not used positively, they become serious obstacles which dramatically limit our ability to achieve our goals. In many cases, people don't realise their Original Dream Intention, and consciously or unconsciously succumb to the Dark Knight until they die. As Wayne Bennett said: 'What are you feeding?' Also, you might find it helpful to remember that there are a range of possible outcomes for every situation; we often spend a lot of time and energy worrying about an outcome that never actually happens.

In the following chapters, we'll look at each Knight in turn.

CHAPTER SUMMARY

1. We continue to seek happiness in external gratifications, even though this always fails.

2. To realise our Dreams, we must resist our thirsts and cravings, and learn to effectively utilise the Five Dark Knights.

CALL TO ACTION

As a young child, you may have felt free to embrace life in its splendour, unaware of the obstacles you will endure. As your mind develops, you sometimes experience rapturous feelings of ecstasy. Complete delight and satisfaction. You want these feelings again, and again, and again. A craving begins. Suffering begins. This process has created the ravenous appetite of the Five Dark Knights. This process can debilitate you, but it is also the doorway to your freedom. Only through understanding, and eventually overcoming your cravings, will you attain happiness and freedom.

CHAPTER 10

THE FIRST DARK KNIGHT – LAZINESS

Laziness is not necessarily what it seems: you can be very active and still achieve the goal of being lazy.

This was an obstacle for me. For the majority of my life, I lived with my parents – they are wonderful human beings! They drove me around to different sporting events so I could fulfil my athletic potential; they taught me admirable life values which I'll take to the grave; they were always supportive mentally, financially and emotionally; and they maintained their patience and belief in me even through the difficult times (and there were plenty). The list could go on! I wouldn't be who I am today without my parents.

But the simple fact is, I was treated like a king when I lived at home. All my meals were made, my washing was done, my car was always clean and the house was always spotless. I did help with the cleaning, but you get the picture – many things were done for me. My only responsibilities were to study and to consciously go after my Dream. I was very lucky.

When Magdalena and I began our life together, I was faced with a situation in which the fundamental duties of life – washing, cooking and cleaning – became my responsibility with Magdalena. The days of being a king were over.

My parents and I maintained our house like a museum; I was accustomed to impeccable tidiness. Magdalena, in comparison (again, an opposite!), doesn't put the same emphasis on her environment. So, I had a dilemma. Who was going to maintain the living standards I was accustomed to? Who was going to prepare the meals? Me, of course.

I realised that I'd become reliant on the high living standard provided by my parents. Most importantly, the time I valued the most was my relaxation time, when I had no duties to perform. Relaxing time was the pinnacle of life for me! Can you see what happened here? The Dark Knight of Laziness had been created because of my upbringing and my living environment.

In my current home with Magdalena, I spend most days wandering around the house trying to maintain the standards I was brought up with – so I can rest! So I can be lazy! My motivation for cleaning is to be able to rest. What the Dark Knight of Laziness doesn't know is that there will always be something to clean. A clean home is impermanent: there will never be a time when everything is done and I can rest. That's an illusion.

The Dark Knight is trying to recapture my childhood experiences in my present life. It found a so-called 'peace' in doing nothing, and it hasn't abandoned those experiences. It received such great enjoyment in watching films and relaxing; therefore, it identified those experiences as 'happiness', and is unwilling to relinquish them.

The Dark Knight of Laziness can also come in the form of lazy thoughts and excuses to avoid change. It's looking for security: 'Oh, I can't be bothered to find a new job. I've had this job for fifteen years, I get paid a good salary, and it's secure. It's too hard to rewrite my curriculum vitae – I'll stay where I am.'

The Dark Knight of Laziness is looking for happiness in comfort, and will avoid challenges. What it doesn't understand is that happiness can be found in the unknown. The Sri Lankan Buddhist monk always highlighted the responsibility of an individual to distinguish between eternal and finite realities. For example: change is an eternal reality. All things that exist will change. But if you purchase a brand-new car and it makes you feel wonderful, those wonderful feelings will eventually disappear. They are finite, and vulnerable to negative influences. Therefore, change is a good investment into your future, because you know it will happen. An eternal reality is absolute, and cannot be influenced by the Dark Knights or any other destructive forces. An example is causality (cause and effect) – see chapter 7. Whatever you give energy to will grow. If you love your garden, and you look after it, your flowers will eventually flourish. Consequently, you can make a very good prediction and therefore find security in the unknown, because you know that wherever you invest your time daily will pay dividends.

What you do every day, will build into tomorrow!

EXERCISE 22: EXAMINING YOUR THOUGHTS OF AVOIDANCE

In the first column of the table on page 131, record the areas of your life in which you either try to avoid your commitments or where you search for security. When do you find yourself desperately wanting unnecessary rest? Please be honest.

Now write the opposite thoughts in the second column. The opposite thoughts will often involve taking a shortcut that may seem like a good idea but doesn't work in reality.

Example situation: A mother dearly loves her eighteen year old son. Knowing that he loves to gamble, she decides to pay his rent for the next six months in order to relieve his monthly expenses and give him financial independence.

The paradox: Unfortunately the son sees his mother's generosity as an opportunity to splurge on the horses. He spends all his income and his mother's rental money with his losses. His future financial security remains even more uncertain.

The opposite thoughts: A mother dearly loves her eighteen-year old son. Knowing that he loves to gamble, she decides to restrict access to his bank account so he doesn't over withdraw it. He borrows money from a friend in order to gamble.

The paradox: The son resents his mother's attempt to stop him gambling and borrows even more money from his friend.

Possible middle path solution: The mother identifies that her son's love of horses is partly driving his gambling, and she advises him to develop a career in horse racing. Her son eventually has a wellpaid career which he loves, and he has enough money to secure his financial future. He no longer feels the urge or the financial need to gamble.

Possible paradox meaning (see chapter 4 for an introduction to paradox meanings): The mother's investment to protect her son from being financially destroyed by his attraction to gambling only created more uncertainty. Now he works in the horse-racing industry but no longer feels the need to gamble.

Her original aim was to give him financial independence. She identified a possible middle path solution, and now he has a lucrative career that he loves.

Example situation: Currently your work does not satisfy you. You have always dreamt about becoming a writer, but you are afraid to reduce your working hours and begin your book, because you will lose income.

The paradox: The company you work for goes bankrupt, you lose your job and income. Now you have plenty of time to write your book, and discover your ideal career; although, your financial future is not secure.

The opposite thoughts: You decide to quit your job and apply for unemployment benefits so you can fully concentrate on your book.

The paradox: You struggle to focus on your writing because you are worried about meeting your financial commitments, so you end up taking another full-time job. With so much to learn in your new position, there is now even less time for writing during your time off.

Possible middle path solutions: You find a new part-time job that pays the rent, and gives you enough time to write your book. Your book becomes a success, and your writing eventually generates as much income as your old job, plus now you're doing something you love.

Or: You stay in your full-time job because your family can't do without any drop in your income, and you commit to writing a realistic number of words a week. Within a year you have formed a writing circle and are getting vital feedback on your first draft. Now you enjoy your day job more because you have committed to a regular writing practice in your own time. Your happiness impacts on your family.

Possible paradox meaning:

Your sense of well-being and your income can increase beyond your imagination, if you love what you do.

Thoughts of avoidance	The opposite thoughts

Your middle path solutions:

What is the paradox meaning, or personal lesson, to take away from this exercise?

CHAPTER SUMMARY

- Laziness looks to comfort for happiness, rather than challenges.
- Happiness can be found in the unknown.

CALL TO ACTION

Finding false comfort in the familiar can ultimately result in depression. Perhaps you thought you were making the sensible choice by taking the safe option? But really you were prolonging the inevitable. Nothing is permanent. Your life is in a constant flux of change, and even though your past experiences gave you joy, it is impossible to perfectly recapture the same moments again. If happiness is what you seek, it may be found in the unknown.

ACTION STEPS

Step 1: This is an action plan that requires you to be very honest with yourself.

Choose a situation in which you are avoiding taking action, or exhibiting lazy behaviour. For example, each time you research new career paths on different recruitment websites, you experience feelings of anxiety and a fear of the unknown – specially with your financial security and responsibilities. You decide to continue with your unfulfilling work. It is safe and pays well.

Step 2: Now write down the opposite of this behaviour. You have been considering resigning from your current job because it doesn't satisfy your career goals anymore. The work is monotonous and you are not utilising all your skills. You dedicate every spare moment to finding the right job for you, which feels like a job in itself. This causes you an unbelievable amount of stress and anxiety.

Step 3: Reconcile the two opposites by finding a middle path solution. Create a safe but challenging action plan. Divide the action plan into slow attainable steps with dates and results. This is a difficult exercise, so practice good self-care. Remember, there is no failure, only an improved outcome for yourself.

For example, you are aware that you can't continue this career forever or you will become depressed. Consequently, you commit to a self-accountable action plan where you apply for two new positions each month; while, limiting the amount of time you take to research the job market. Perhaps, after a few months, you will feel able to apply for three positions a month until you find the position you want.

CHAPTER 11

THE SECOND DARK KNIGHT – ENDLESS SEARCHING

The second Dark Knight – endless searching – is obsessive concentration and focus. It's the quality within you that looks for perfection in outward gratification.

My Buddhist friend used the example that when a beehive is attacked, the bees fly around frantically trying to restore their home. They search endlessly for a way to maintain the perfect status quo. Or picture a girl online-shopping for the perfect dress for Saturday's party: she searches and searches and searches, but to no avail. She can't find that perfect dress. She doesn't achieve her goal, because she's too absorbed in the process of searching, never 100 per cent happy with what she finds. This is the essence of the second Dark Knight – searching for perfection in a world of imperfection.

'One of the basic rules of the universe is that nothing is perfect. Perfection simply doesn't exist… Without imperfection, neither you nor I would exist.'

Stephen Hawking

EXERCISE 23: UNCOVERING PERFECTIONISM

Think of a situation in which you exhibited perfectionist behaviour. What did you want to achieve? Why were you searching for perfection?

Now, many people think that perfectionism is positive. You'll hear people say things like, 'I have standards! I'm a 130 per cent person!'

In my time-management course, we often discuss the burden of perfection. Let's look now at a mathematical example from the course to do with personal energy.

Say that my goal is to finish a work project with excellent results. Normally, I need to give 100 per cent energy every day for five days to achieve an excellent result. In other words:

Goal: an excellent result for my project

Outcome: my client's business needs are fulfilled, and I receive another contract

Endless searching is created by the unattainable goal of perfection.

Energy required: 100 per cent

But what if I decided to give, not 100 per cent, but eighty per cent, with the intention of sufficiently fulfilling my client's business needs without being perfect? Would I achieve the same result? Would I have more energy at the end of the week? Your goal for excellence is about you, not the client. Yes, you would like to achieve admirable results which your client appreciates, but the excellence aspect is about answering your self-expectations, and at what cost? Analyse your goals and behaviour, and identify where you are pursuing superfluous goals using unnecessary amounts of energy. Working smarter means working smarter with yourself.

Will the client look for another provider of my service if their business needs are met? Probably not. The effort that it takes to look for a new provider, write contracts and so on, would be too much of a burden. So:

Five days of 100 per cent energy = 500 per cent = my client buys a new contract

OR:

Five days of 80 per cent = 400 per cent = my client *still* buys a new contract

And I save 100 per cent worth of energy for other work or recreational activities.

Please don't misunderstand me. I'm not implying you should drop your standards – I'm saying you can work more efficiently and in a more sustainable manner. Work-life balance is about evenly distributing energy to all aspects of your life – on a day-to-day basis. Your ability to preserve your health depends upon how well you can do this.

Are there different ways to work and live more sustainably with your personal energy? For example, a good strategy for me would be to sit down and re-evaluate my old habits, and see if I can find more effective and efficient ways to keep the house clean.

Another, more specific example: say that it's rubbish collection time and I have to take the bin out. I could go downstairs now; if I do, the house will be free of rubbish and I can continue my movie. But I know that Magdalena would like to go out in two hours. So I'll be going downstairs in two hours anyway. Doesn't it make sense to refrain from perfectionism and not take the rubbish out now, but wait until we leave? Surely walking downstairs once is more efficient than twice?

I know this is a simple example, but it drives home the point. You don't have to be perfect to be effective – and anyway, you can't be perfect, because we live in an imperfect universe.

EXERCISE 24: HOW CAN YOU LIVE WITH LESS PERFECTIONISM?

Jot down some ideas for ways in which you could live more sustainably.

Perfection is an illusion. It does not exist.
When you strive to achieve it, you're being motivated
by your failures, not your achievements.

EXERCISE 25: RETHINKING PERFECTIONISM

Now, please reanalyse the situation you recorded in exercise 23, where you exhibited perfectionist behaviour. Is it possible to achieve the same result with less energy? Please remember, the end result is impermanent!

CHAPTER SUMMARY

1. Perfection is an unattainable goal, meaning we can search for it endlessly.

2. It's impossible to achieve perfection in an impermanent existence.

3. Perfection doesn't exist: it's an illusion.

4. When we strive for perfection, we're being motivated by our failures, not our successes.

CALL TO ACTION

Perfectionism is: trying to fill a glass to the top with sand, which has a huge hole in the bottom of it. It is impossible! Whatever your motivation is to reach perfection, you are fighting a battle you cannot win. Perfection is a final result, in a world where there are NO final results. Why? Because the result will CHANGE! It is impermanent. Please analyse your motivations for perfection and realise that the only way you can achieve an excellent result is to do the best you can, and accept the imperfection of the result!

ACTION STEPS

Step 1: Evaluate situations where you exhibit perfectionistic behaviour.

Step 2: Prioritise your situations, and choose the highest priority situation where your energy is being most depleted. In the left column, note your behaviour, motives for the behaviour, and how much energy you think you are using (a little? A lot?) measured by time and effort. In the right column, for the same situation, note your options for alternative behaviour that you can sustain, and your thoughts on how much energy you can save overall (a little or a lot?). The idea is to find an alternative approach that will ultimately achieve the same result but will also put less pressure on you.

FOR EXAMPLE:

Perfectionist behaviour

You spend months reviewing architectural drawings to renovate your house. It is a high-priority project because your wife is expecting your second child in a few months. You don't have a bedroom in your house for the new child. You want to create the space before he or she is born so that you can focus on the baby. However, none of the architect's suggestions are exactly what you want.

Motive

To embrace this lifetime opportunity and create your dream home.

Paradox meaning

You are frustrated by your lack of progress and your family are finding it hard to communicate with you. You continue to research the options and your wife accuses you of being unsupportive.

Alternative behaviour

Put the project on hold until your child is older. They won't need their own bedroom for several years. That way you can focus on your partner and prepare for the birth without distractions.

OR:

Commit to a proposal that encapsulates most of your dream-home vision. Ask for a clause that will enable the builder to be flexible with any minor details you are uncertain about. Get the project started.

Sustainable motive

Make sure the project gets underway so that you can reduce your family's stress levels and focus on your new baby. Befriend your builder and stay open to new ideas, and remember you can always change things if you are not happy with the results.

Step 3: Perfectionism resolution: compare the two columns and decide on an alternative behaviour which is sustainable, but can achieve the same result(s).

EXERCISE 26: PERFECTIONISM ACTION PLAN

Perfectionistic behaviour	**Alternative behaviour**
Motive	Sustainable motive
How much energy you will use	How much energy you can save

Perfectionism resolution:

CHAPTER 12

THE THIRD DARK KNIGHT – DOUBT

'There is nothing more dreadful than the habit of doubt. Doubt separates people. It is a poison that disintegrates friendships and breaks up pleasant relations. It is a thorn that irritates and hurts; it is a sword that kills.'

Dwight Goddard, *Buddha, Truth and Brotherhood: An Epitome of Many Buddhist Scriptures,* translated from the Japanese

Doubt and self-doubt are very similar. Doubt is questioning a set of circumstances outside of yourself, and self-doubt is questioning your ability to behave in a certain way.

What can self-doubt lead to?

- Anger
- Disillusionment
- The breakdown of relationships
- Violence
- Resentment.

And this is only the tip of the iceberg.

Everyone has experienced the third Dark Knight. Doubt is a powerfully vicious level of 'concentration' which can undermine and ruin relationships and achievements. Doubt diverts us from honourable thought processes such as belief and trust. Would Eve have eaten the apple if she hadn't doubted the original instructions from God? At work you have recently employed a young university student to help around the office. Your manager and colleagues dismiss the student's capability to take on difficult tasks because of her minimal experience. Two weeks later, the student and you are doing overtime to reach an urgent deadline. You are confused, and can't find a solution to a particular problem. The student sees your dilemma, intervenes and solves your problem in five minutes. How much of the student's potential is not being utilised because your colleagues judged and doubted her?

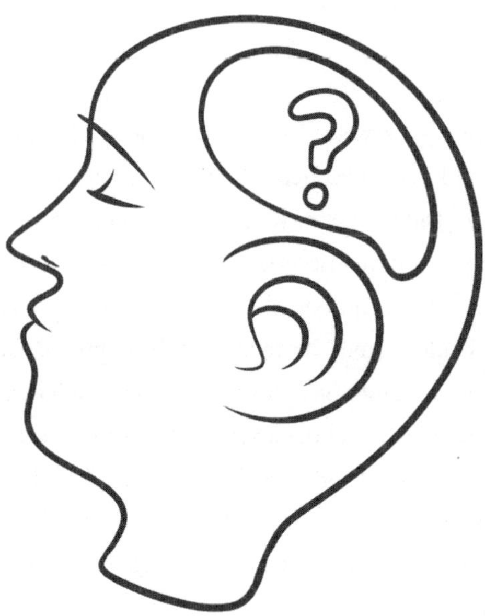

Doubt can change your life forever, so it's important to guard against it.

Explaining why a person doubts something or someone is not my goal in this chapter. Remember our icebergs are very deep and complex.

Let's take a look at three things that can eliminate doubt from your mind: belief, dedication and trust.

BELIEF

'Keep your dreams alive. Understand to achieve anything requires faith and belief in yourself, vision, hard work, determination, and dedication. Remember all things are possible for those who believe.'

Retired track and field athlete Gail Devers

Belief is very much a synonym for other honourable thought processes such as faith and certitude. Belief is your capacity to trust in a set of circumstances outside of yourself, and self-belief is how much you trust your own ability to behave in a certain way. Belief has spurred great people to unimaginable heights, and can defy all odds and give you peace of mind in the most difficult of times. It can also do the opposite, of course. When belief is misguided, history has shown that it can result in genocide.

Each individual experiences a sense of belief differently.

The key word here is purpose – the practical path that emanates from belief and will make doubt seem insignificant. Before we venture on to discussing purpose, however, let's go back to your Original Dream Intention.

YOUR ORIGINAL DREAM INTENTION

Please rewrite your Original Dream Intention in the space below.

....

....

....

....

....

....

Now can you see or feel, in the wording of your Original Dream Intention, the element of belief? Is there a sense of action or movement in your words? For example, say that your intention is 'to help the world achieve a sustainable level of greenhouses gases'. Your wording implies that you believe that it's possible to achieve such a level – and that you're willing to commit your energy and time to help make it a reality.

Your Original Dream Intention comes from a place of belief: a calling or knowing expressed through a 'feeling thought' that feels undeniably right.

Now that your Original Dream Intention is cemented into your consciousness again, let's make a plan. Let's create purpose!

Only through consciously implementing your Original Dream Intention can you create purpose and overcome doubt.

EXERCISE 27: CREATING PURPOSE

Where do you see yourself in three years, after establishing your Original Dream Intention?

What are your short-term goals? What will you achieve in the next six months? How will you know you have achieved those goals? Will you have the capacity to attain your goal?

What kind of people do you need to contact to achieve your goals? How will you contact them? Telephone calls, emails, door-knocking?

What weekly and monthly actions will help you ignite your Original Dream Intention?

By answering these questions you will find purpose through the snowball effect – gaining momentum as you move forward. Each action you perform in service of your Original Dream Intention will give rise to and propel the next action.

DEDICATION AND TRUST

Trust and dedication are connected. You can only be dedicated to a goal if you believe that your goal is the right one for you. When you go through challenging times (and undoubtedly you will), your belief will be tested, and you will only be able to maintain your dedication by trusting in your goal. A very talented tennis player may have lost his last ten professional tennis matches. His confidence is down, he contemplates leaving the professional circuit. Trusting in his own talent can provide an ample amount of determination to overcome his drop in form, and continue playing fantastic tennis.

You need an unbelievable amount of dedication to achieve the Dream – it's a lifelong pursuit that will confront you with good, bad and almost unbearable obstacles. I spent many a day in tears during my time as an actor, wondering, 'Is this path for me?' Doubt is actually a logical step in the process of realising your dreams. And it's okay to doubt yourself!

The Dream is not an unforgiving process, it's the opposite (a paradox). You need sacrifice and courage in order to fulfil your own Dream; that's why it's the embodiment of the greatest love of all, forgiveness. The Dream will provide you with the best possible situation in order to realise it. For example, if you have made some dishonest financial transactions, there will be a consequence for your decision (the Eightfold path: be mindful), but the Dream will also give you an opportunity to redeem yourself. It doesn't hold a grudge against you. It will give you an opportunity to turn your negative choice in a positive one (see chapter 4, Understanding opposites).

I once watched an episode of Oprah Winfrey's *SuperSoul Sunday* called 'The Dhamma Brothers'. ('Dhamma' is another term for 'dharma', which comes from the ancient religions of India and means 'the natural laws of the universe'.) The episode was about prison inmates in an Alabama correctional facility (on death row or serving life) who were introduced to Vipassana with a ten-day meditation retreat. Even murderers and rapists can access the forgiving qualities of the Dream – nobody is exempt. During and after the retreat, the inmates' behaviour was assessed. Even though some inmates regressed, the majority exhibited increased levels of tolerance and compassion for others. What is important is that your belief and dedication are based on your Original Dream Intention, then they'll be stronger than doubt, and anything the other four Dark Knights can conjure. With trust in yourself, you can overcome all obstacles, even though you may not think so at the time.

You'll fail many times as you follow the Dream, and that's okay. Failure is a catalyst! And never forget: you can't truly experience success without knowing how failure feels. Turning negatives into positives, and reconciling the opposites, as we discussed in chapter 4, is the source of your power. I want to make two final important points about trust and dedication.

1. **Firstly: trust is based on the big picture.** When times get tough, it's important that you return to your Original Dream Intention. Only by trusting in the legitimacy of your original intention can you defend yourself against the Five Dark Knights.

2. **Secondly: dedication is fuelled by momentum** (ie noting your successes, however small you consider them to be, and your ability to find the positive in every situation). During my youth I had a severe speech impediment, which I was treated for with limited success. When we read aloud during English class in high school, I would stammer my way through paragraphs in front

of the whole class. It was a humiliating experience. My way of coping was through avoidance (the First Dark Knight – laziness). When we began to read in English class, I would go to the toilet just before it was my turn to read, and sit there for five minutes waiting for my turn to pass. I was terrified of experiencing that humiliation.

I'm now a motivational speaker. My job is to speak in public and teach English! Through dedication, you too can turn your weaknesses into your greatest strengths – and each positive, courageous step you take will build your momentum. As you break through each of your personal barriers, you'll discover a power manifesting inside you that will allow you to overcome the next obstacle. The stronger you become, the greater the obstacles: each obstacle will propel you into the next challenge as you become a Warrior of Light (see *Manual of the Warrior of Light* by Paulo Coelho).

CHAPTER SUMMARY

1. Your Original Dream Intention comes from a place of belief – it's a calling or a knowing.

2. You create purpose and dispel doubt only by following your Original Dream Intention.

3. Trust is based on the big picture.

4. Dedication is fuelled by your successes and attempts to find the positive in all situations.

CALL TO ACTION

You are extraordinary. You are unique. You have a specific purpose in this world. This purpose has been designed to balance your strengths and weaknesses in order to complement each other. When you identify your Original Dream Intention, know that in your heart, your feeling thoughts are undeniable. They are the truth. (Remember that a feeling thought has a simultaneous reaction in your mind and body. Other thoughts are only in your mind.) Once you receive this confirmation, use your Original Dream Intention as your source of motivation in all situations from this day forward. Realise your destiny, and become who you truly are.

ACTION STEPS

Step 1: Where do you encounter doubt or self-doubt in your life? Please write them down.

Step 2: Self-analyse why you question the situations or yourself in the situations. Write your doubts or self-doubts down. Please try and be completely honest with yourself. The Dark Knight Doubt will throw excuses and so-called rationale your way to justify your doubts.

Step 3: Now return to your Original Dream Intention. Compare it to your doubts page. What do you see? Are these two pages compatible? If not, how can you turn the negative – your doubts – into a positive – your Original Dream Intention? It is ok when you feel helpless. There is no pressure on you to do anything. But know that your doubts are debilitating your Original Dream Intention. In a safe and careful way, turn your doubts into thoughts of belief, dedication and trust. Practically implement exercise 27: Creating purpose. The world is a classroom. It is a place to try new things. There is no failure. Only new experiences.

CHAPTER 13

THE FOURTH DARK KNIGHT – BLAME

Each Dark Knight is a 'concentration level' – a way of thinking through your perception, prejudices, experiences and so on. Blame has the capacity to cause physical harm: whether you blame yourself or others, blame can lead to aggression or even violence.

Why do we blame others? Because we believe our opinion is correct and theirs is not? Because of misunderstandings? Due to lack of awareness of others' motives and situations? Because we don't want to take responsibility for fear of the consequences? Because our personal agenda has been compromised?

All of the above.

BLAME – A DEFENCE MECHANISM

This fourth Dark Knight defends the agendas of the other Knights and of the network as a whole. It's an aggressive knight with a short fuse. Magdalena regularly confronts me about my personal agendas, and most of the time my first reaction is to point the finger and say, 'But what about you?'

The Knight of Blame has been in action all over the world, from the ancient wars to the present. Men and women have murdered, destroyed, savaged, crucified, assassinated, executed and annihilated to protect themselves and their agendas. Since the beginning of history, blame has been prevalent among human beings. But why? Why do we repeat this cycle over and over again?

As I said, this fourth Dark Knight is a reactionary one: it serves the other knights. If we want to understand it, we need to know what it's protecting and why. A Dark Knight can easily be summoned unintentionally, and the Dark Knights use blame to protect themselves from the middle path – see chapter 4, Understanding opposites. Let's look at this in a logical way. We've analysed three of the Five Dark Knights so far – laziness, endless searching and doubt. If we become aware of and stop ourselves from being lazy, endlessly searching and feeling doubtful, is it possible that the Dark Knight of blame will have nothing to protect? The gatekeepers can't protect the castle if the castle is no longer there, after all. It would be easy to say, 'Let's just eliminate the Dark Knights, and we'll no longer have problems. We can live our lives in freedom and enjoyment.'

Very easy to say, but to do? That's another story.

My Buddhist monk friend indicated to me that it's always possible for fear to resurface. Even if you defend against the Dark Knights for a long time, their illusions can still be reactivated by external or internal influences. A good example of this is my obsessive-compulsive disorder (OCD). Throughout my life, my OCD has fluctuated. When I have minimal stress in my life for three or four months, it's less intense – but when I'm attached to future or past fears, it's reactivated almost at full strength.

If you slip into the past or future, you enter the domain of the Dark Knights. The Dream demands that you focus on the 'now'.

There are many books that focus on how to stay in the present, but one in particular stands out for me: Eckhart Tolle's *The Power of Now: A guide to spiritual enlightenment*. Tolle is a world leader in spiritual development and has influenced the hearts and minds of millions around the world. Obviously, the main focus of the book is the importance of embodying the present moment. I believe Mr Tolle is absolutely correct in this, but I'm also aware of the relentless bombardment of the Dark Knights' illusions. It's difficult! 'Being in the now' is our doorway to salvation and the fulfilment of the Dream, yes, but we still have to take the journey step by step.

YOUR DEFENCE AGAINST BLAME – NOT REACTING

Over the years of my battle with OCD, I've done a large amount of research to find ways to deal with it. One key piece of advice I received was, 'Never react to the voices.' One major obstacle a person with OCD has is that they believe the negative voices in their head are real. They are not you! As mentioned in chapter 9, we experience eternal and finite realities. The negative self-talk dialogue in your mind is finite. A very simple example: your colleague seems upset with you. You wonder, what did you do wrong? When the time is right, you confront your colleague about their behaviour, and ask why are they being so insensitive? Your colleague quickly apologises and explains that they are preoccupied with a difficult project at the moment. It had nothing to do with you! But your negative self-talk dialogue believed it was real because it was influenced by your perception: a mixture of logic, facts, emotions, feelings, personal interpretations and prejudices. Your negative self-talk dialogue is vulnerable to questionable influences.

This is the key to subduing the Dark Knights and not allowing blame (or violence) to dominate. Which wolf are you feeding? Is it possible to reduce the number of times you react to the Dark Knights and slowly build your resilience to them? You can also build your resilience level by practicing Vipassana (see chapter 3).

Only through not reacting can you silence the Dark Knights and stop blame from surfacing. If you fight the Dark Knights, you only give them greater impetus to influence you further.

It's possible. I've built my personal resilience to drinking alcohol, for example. As a young man, I enjoyed a drink or three; when I met Magdalena, I still had my little party times but they became less frequent. My wife doesn't like excessive drinking and we had a few strong disagreements on the topic. I gradually recognised the unnecessary nature of binge-drinking, even if it was only on a night out with the boys once every six months.

There were three important aspects to my transformation:

1. **I never said, 'I won't binge-drink again.'** Identifying with the opposite behaviour to the one you're changing will only suppress your urges.

2. **Consequences change behaviour.** I value my happiness with Magdalena more than binge-drinking: the idea of losing her over it was a powerful motivation.

3. **Over time, I built resilience to the desire.** After not participating in binge-drinking over a long period, I no longer have the urge to do so.

Not reacting over an extended period of time allowed me to build a resilience which protected me from the Dark Knights.

If you can accept every situation and remove your own agenda, you will be free. For example: if you come home after a long day at work, and you expect your partner to have cooked dinner, and they haven't, you will be disappointed. You have made the assumption that a future event will occur, instead of staying open to what will happen. Note: in saying acceptance is the key, I'm certainly not suggesting that you accept unreasonable behaviour from others. I believe in assertiveness and in stating your position to others, and that all parties should respect others' opinions. However, you can accept the situation by showing tolerance, not judging, and stating your point of view without biases or ulterior motives.

EXERCISE 28: DEFENDING YOURSELF AGAINST BLAME

Are you currently behaving in a way that you have no control over in specific situations? If yes, what are they?

If you could behave differently, what would you do?

What would be the logical compromise for these opposite behaviours? Is there a middle path to be found by accepting your own behaviour and another's and creating a 'win/win' situation?

Do you currently have a habit that you feel you have no control over?

....

....

....

....

Consequences change people's behaviour. What's the consequence of your current behaviour?

....

....

....

....

....

How could you build your resilience to this habit? What's a realistic six-month plan that won't create stress for you?

....

....

....

....

Note: There is no judgement or pressure in the process of changing your personal behaviour. Realising the Dream is all about forgiveness. So please be honest with yourself and change dangerous behaviour(s) slowly.

CHAPTER SUMMARY

1. Realising your Dream means that you must focus on the present; the past and future are the domain of the Dark Knights.

2. Only by not reacting – by accepting a situation – can you silence the Dark Knights and prevent blame.

CALL TO ACTION

Blame is the bodyguard for the other four Dark Knights. It is trying to protect illusions. When you point the finger at another, your intention is to protect something of value to you, because you are afraid to lose it. Would you blame that person if you didn't value your idea or belief? Probably not. If you arrive at the point where you need to be aggressive in order to achieve your objective, then what you are protecting is not being protected. You are only irritating the situation by increasing the likelihood of further harm to you, or the thing you are protecting. Don't react to provocation, become proactive, and look for achievable solutions and compromises.

ACTION STEPS

Step 1: Take a moment to reflect on situations in the past where you have had a short fuse.

Step 2: Analyse what you were protecting during those situations, and why? Are the things that you protected important now? Did you achieve a positive outcome for you, and the other person or people in the situations?

Step 3: Close your eyes, choose one dangerous situation from step 2 and imagine it is recurring in the future. This situation is becoming very volatile and if it goes unchecked, could have a disastrous consequence for all people involved. How would you react differently this time? What would be an optimal win-win solution for everyone? How can you accept responsibility for your actions and empathise with the other person or people involved? Please remember: one reflex action of blame can permanently damage a relationship.

CHAPTER 14

THE FIFTH DARK KNIGHT – DESIRE

In the last few hundred years (and as a direct result of the industrial revolution), some key facets of society have evolved:

- Individuals express their opinions more readily.
- Mass literacy and media have snowballed.
- Independent social groups have evolved from authoritarian governments.
- Science and technology have dramatically impacted on global culture and communication.
- Urban populations have multiplied.
- Representative democracy has been set in motion globally.
- Industrialisation has proliferated.
- And desire – the craving for external stimuli – has increased.

Desire has been a strong motivator for humans throughout all the ages. Here's the definition according to Wikipedia:

> *'Desire is a sense of longing or hoping for a person, object, or outcome. The same sense is expressed by emotions such as 'craving'. When a person desires something or someone, their sense of longing is excited*

by the enjoyment or the thought of the item or person, and they want to take actions to obtain their goal.'

My Sri Lankan brother called it 'The need for desire.' In other words, the need to have an unattainable object of desire.

The fifth Dark Knight is desire and here are its synonyms:

admiration	fervour	need
ambition	fondness	passion
appetite	frenzy	predilection
ardour	greed	proclivity
aspiration	hankering	propensity
attraction	hunger	rapaciousness
avidity	inclination	rapture
concupiscence	infatuation	ravenousness
covetousness	itch	relish
craving	lasciviousness	salacity
craze	lechery	solicitude
cupidity	libido	thirst
devotion	liking	urge
doting	love	voracity
eagerness	lust	will
fancy	mania	wish
fascination	motive	yearning

thesaurus.com

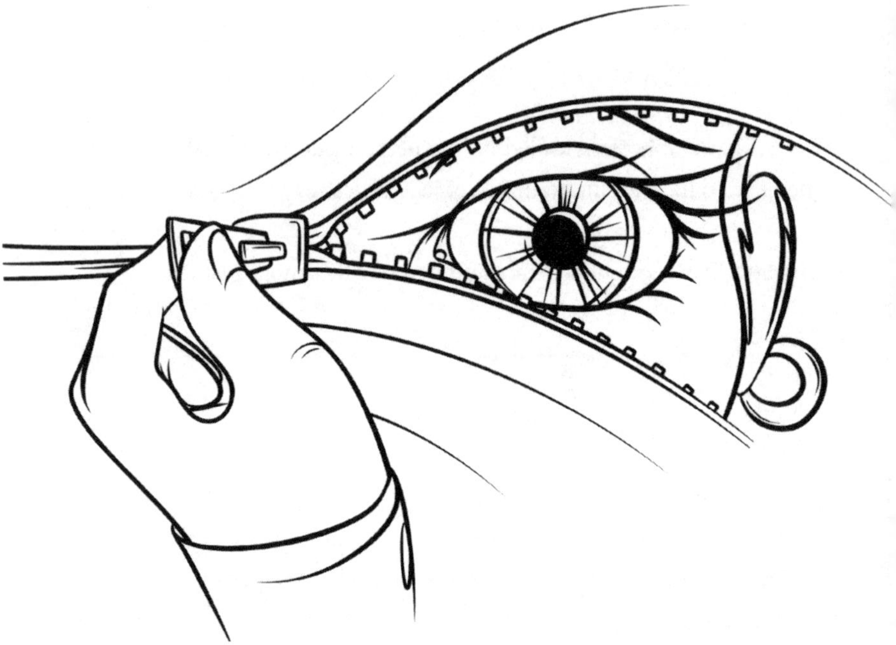

The fifth Dark Knight takes many forms. We mostly associate desire with lust, passion and yearning, but it encompasses any type of desire that is never satisfied for long, whether for chocolate, alcohol, cigarettes, recognition or even happiness. It's that insatiable appetite inside us: always hungry, and always wanting more.

Desire is unavoidable! It's existed forever, but in the twenty-first century, this fifth Dark Knight is shoved, crammed, jammed and thrust into our faces day and night. You can't go anywhere without seeing some type of sexual innuendo, whether it's a beautiful supermodel advertising Calvin Klein underwear or a movie star pitching a new Chanel fragrance. Temptation is around us 24/7.

The fifth Dark Knight is the basic advertising weapon of multinational companies around the world – everyone knows that sex sells products. Whether through explicit porn sites or just in basic advertising, it's everywhere!

The society of the Western world and beyond encourages desire. It uses human weaknesses to fuel the capitalistic machine of consumption – and even the machine itself (the huge multinational companies, Wall Street, our democracies), are slaves to desire. The internet, television and all multimedia technology are only ever a fingertip away. Most of us are constantly on the verge of consuming products, either online or in department stores, that are sold to us in a sexualised manner.

How can we learn to overcome this bombardment of temptation? How can we break free of an urge that will never be satisfied?

OVERCOMING DESIRE – CREATING AWARENESS

There are five things you need to be aware of in order to overcome desire.

FIRST: REMEMBER THAT THE BODY IS NOT ETERNAL, SO YOUR FEELINGS OF DESIRE WILL DIMINISH OVER TIME.

The most important fact to recognise is that the fifth Dark Knight works in the realm of the body and its senses. Desire is trying to achieve happiness through sensations: we want to feel contentment, warmth, love and happiness. The fifth Dark Knight takes advantage of these longings to sell us cheap illusions. Desire tells you, 'Eat three chocolate bars. It'll make you happy.' We eat them, and yes, we feel good – but is that the end? No, it's not! You will eventually want more.

Eating chocolate bars repeatedly is a trap: desire has influenced you to seek happiness through external stimuli, and it will keep on doing so. Eating three chocolate bars will not make you happy. It's actually the beginning of suffering, because you're trying to achieve an eternal goal (happiness) using a non-eternal experience (eating chocolate).

SECOND: DESIRE HAS THE ABILITY TO BREAK DOWN YEARS OF HARD WORK IN A SECOND.

Let's consider an alcoholic who has been sober for ten years as an example. She or he has a terribly painful experience, and feels the need to drink. After a few minutes of contemplation, she or he falls off the wagon – ten years down the drain for a few minutes of 'happiness'. The alcoholic could refrain from drinking, though, if he or she were aware that this desire will pass – it's only temporary. A colleague and very good friend of mine once said, 'A thought is like a cloud in the sky: it appears as quickly as it disappears.'

Desire also works in reverse. Say you have a wonderful night in a new outfit you just bought. You're complimented by friends on how great you look. For years afterwards, you buy clothes with the subconscious aim to relive that night, looking for those feelings of recognition. But are those feelings of recognition temporary or permanent? Is it possible to realise that and change your redundant behaviour through the second Noble Truth, *samudāya* (which we talked about in chapter 8)? Your thirsts and cravings will disappear in a temporary, conditional, changing world. If you know your feelings will change, then you don't have to hold on to them.

THIRD: THE FIVE DARK KNIGHTS WORK IN PARTNERSHIP. THEY'RE A NETWORK.

A partnership that commonly forms within the Five Dark Knights is between the Dark Knight of desire and the second Dark Knight of endless searching. As with the example of the outfit we just discussed, when we have a wonderful experience of the senses our natural tendency is to try to relive it. We somehow think that by doing so we'll have the same feelings as before. Thus begins an endless and futile search to recapture the original experience – but your feelings aren't eternal, so it's impossible for any experience to be exactly the same.

I know it's very easy to say, 'Accept the experience for what it was and move on.' It's difficult to implement, though, especially when your motive is subconscious. But it's the only way to cease the endless searching.

Another example of how the Five Dark Knights can work together is adultery. If one person in a relationship becomes unsatisfied with their partner, their natural instinct is to search for a new partner with a better understanding of their needs. The fifth Dark Knight, desire, is working with the third Dark Knight, doubt, and the original relationship may be destroyed.

Again, is it possible to identify that these feelings of discontentment are temporary? Before the person decides to make a rash decision, they could discuss these temporary feelings with their partner. Remember what we said in chapter 4: 'One negative thought turns into a bigger negative thought, which turns into an even bigger negative thought.' If you make a decision to have an affair, who will get hurt? Your partner, yourself *and* the person you have the affair with! And did you achieve your goal of overcoming your feelings of discontentment? No!

Of course, seeking a new partner may be the correct step if the relationship has become destructive and unhealthy. In this case the couple should separate, but with positive, well-thought-out decisions, not rash ones based on changeable feelings. But perhaps the couple can resolve their differences and stay together.

FOURTH: THE PURITY OF YOUR INTENTION WILL PROTECT YOU FROM DESIRE.

The purity of your intention influences the beginning and end result of your behaviour. It may not be easy to recognise, but your goal and its success depends upon the authenticity of your original intention, and whether it was based on love or fear.

The intentions behind your everyday actions function in exactly the same way as your Original Dream Intention. What you intend is what you'll receive. So, if your intention is to seek personal fulfilment and escapism in an affair, that's what you'll receive. But what will that actually bring you? A few months of exciting lovemaking followed by – what? A lifetime of heartache and pain for your spouse, yourself and your children, if you have any?

Satisfying your physical desires is a short-term method of fulfilment. It doesn't solve any problems: it creates more. Let's say you bought a brand-new car – how long will it really satisfy you? What if the car gets damaged, what then? The simple fact is, investing your happiness in areas that are vulnerable to change is a recipe for disaster.

What is motivating you? Is it desire? Or is it connected to your Original Dream Intention? How 'pure' your behaviour is refers to whether you give to others rather than considering what's in it for you. Is your behaviour self-centred, or selfless? Can you honestly and confidently say your intention is to generally help others? Or does it depend on the situation?

I have already mentioned in chapter 5 that I attended parties with the intention of finding my soulmate or a like-minded woman to share my life with. This was a self-centred desire focused on my emotional needs. What was the outcome? I went home empty-handed. When I met Magdalena, my only intention was to enjoy myself, and see where the moment took us. What was the result? I found a soulmate to share my life with.

If your intention in a specific situation is to fulfil a personal agenda without considering the recipient(s) of your behaviour, you could eventually experience pushback and rejection. Subsequently, your personal agenda will not be achieved.

EXERCISE 29: ASSESSING WHETHER YOUR INTENTION IS PURE

What current situation is causing you pain?

....

....

....

....

....

....

....

....

....

....

....

Think about your original intention for the situation. Is there any evidence that a self-centred desire motivated your behaviour? If yes, what was it?

If you have identified a self-centred desire, what behaviour could you change? How could you refocus your attention on the wellbeing of all people in the situation, including yourself? What inspirational verbs and adjectives could you use in order to redefine your intention?

What will the personal consequences be if you don't change your self-centred desire?

FIFTH: USE YOUR SENSES TO YOUR ADVANTAGE.

The fifth and final awareness way to defend yourself from desire is meditation. We highlighted how life-changing this could be in chapter 3 on Vipassana. Simply returning to observe your breath in a given moment can instantly eliminate the Five Dark Knights and their torturous thoughts.

Sitting is the most effective posture in which to meditate, but there are others. You can also, for example, meditate through movement. I'm not referring to yoga or tai chi here – everything we do can be a type of meditation! Since desire is attached to your senses, why not use your senses to increase your awareness and silence the Five Dark Knights?

Here are four examples of how to refocus your thoughts using movement and your senses:

1. As you walk, feel how each foot touches the ground. Begin with the heel and follow the sensation to your toes. Try to focus on the details of your observations. This will enhance the results of your meditation.

2. If your mind is torturing you with thoughts of desire, simply take two or three deep breaths. Then spend two minutes observing the transference of breath from your nostrils to your top lip.

3. Touch an inanimate or natural (and preferably not human) object. Run your fingers over the surface of the object. By doing this, you can ground your thoughts and find stillness.

4. Listen to the sounds around you. Increasing your awareness of sound replaces a destructive thought pattern (desire) with a constructive thought pattern (observation).

These meditation techniques are fantastic because they can be done anywhere, at any time of the day. Just use the technique that works best for you when your thoughts become unbearable. Or even better, create a habit of meditation at a specific time of day or night and build your resilience to the Dark Knights. Be proactive!

* * *

This second part of the book has been a big one. I hope you aren't overwhelmed by our discussion of the obstacles your Dream faces. Remember the Five Dark Knights are the catalysts of your freedom. They don't know it, but the knights exist in a pair of opposites belonging to the paradox called 'happiness'.

The Dark Knights believe they'll find happiness in non-eternal experiences: it really is a tragedy. They need your help! And only through understanding the thoughts of the Five Dark Knights can you achieve your dreams and true internal and external happiness. It's a paradox! Remember the Buddhist concept that we are born into suffering.

CHAPTER SUMMARY

1. The body isn't eternal, so your desires will diminish.

2. Giving in to a desire can break down years of hard work in a second.

3. The Five Dark Knights work together.

4. The purity of your Original Dream Intention will protect you from desire.

5. Use your senses to your advantage, through meditation.

CALL TO ACTION

It is not easy to resist something that feels so good. You experienced an intensely delightful thrilling feeling, and your mind invites you to consume it again. It lures and seduces you. It persuades you to believe it can provide the same euphoric feeling AGAIN! But it can't. Your mind can only provide the process of WANTING that feeling, but never achieving it again. It is sad. It is torture.

All euphoric feelings are temporary feelings that will disappear. If you become vulnerable to your desires, please focus on the big picture and ask this question: 'Is this feeling eternal or temporary? Will it be with me in the morning, or will it be gone?' If the feeling is eternal, then embrace it. If it is temporary – be careful, because it can cause you a lot of suffering.

ACTION STEPS

Step 1: In what situations do you feel vulnerable to your desires? Is it the late-night sweets in front of the television? Or do you have an extreme fitness programme because you desire an unbelievable body? Please be honest with yourself, and write down a list of your insatiable desires.

Step 2: Choose a desire from your list that you would like to overcome. Please find a quiet area, sit in the Vipassana meditation position, and visualise yourself consuming the desire. Then visualise a consequence to your indulgence. Then do it again, but this time the consequence grows. Do this process twenty times. For example: if you are binge-eating chocolate imagine your teeth decaying, until by the time you reach the twentieth binge your teeth start to drop out.

Step 3: Maintain your meditation position and visualise yourself allowing the desires to go through you, but don't react. Then do it again. Do this twenty times, Each time you accumulate more and more strength. How do you feel now?

Please remember: The body is not eternal. The feelings of gratification that the fifth Dark Knight longs for will eventually cause you pain if left unchecked. Be smart and think of the people whom you love. Think of the big picture.

CHAPTER 15

REDEFINE YOUR ORIGINAL DREAM INTENTION

EXERCISE 30: YOUR ORIGINAL DREAM INTENTION

Please redefine your Original Dream Intention and your Dream to see what if anything has changed since chapter 1. What have you learnt about yourself and your priorities? What do you need to focus on in the weeks and months ahead?

CONCLUSION

Writing *The Dream* has been a thought-provoking and astonishing experience for me. Through reflecting on my own path through life, I have re-learnt the power and brilliance of the Dream.

My primary reason for writing this book, however, was to help others to attain their dreams. I hope it has helped you find that special spark inside of you. There's no one in this world who is exactly like you – you have something very special to give that no one else can, and it would be a tragedy if the world didn't benefit from your gifts. I offer this book to you with open hands, and hope we meet again.

Here's to your dreams!

Through the imperfections of reality,
we can discover the perfection of the Dream.

Grant Rodney Kitchen

ACKNOWLEDGEMENTS

REDDOOR PUBLISHING

A special thank you to Clare Christian and the RedDoor team. Thank you for believing in and sharing the Dream with the world.

MAGDALENA SCHEX

To my wife, best friend, and soulmate. You are my muse, and without you, nothing is possible.

ROD AND KAY KITCHEN

Your unconditional support is the backbone to my dream. Thank you for embracing every twist and turn with your love and generosity.

VANESSA BATTERSBY

You took the Dream to a new level and created opportunities with your expertise and professionalism. Thank you.

MICHELLE RUSHTON AND SHAUN KENNY

In the very early stages, your guidance, know-how and emotional support were the stepping stones that made the Dream a reality.

CHRISTA AND GERD SCHEX

Your day-to-day leadership allows Magdalena and I to achieve our potential – regardless of each obstacle we encounter.

MEHGAWANNA GURUGE

My dear brother, thank you for sharing Buddha's teachings, and allowing me to realise my own conclusions.

For more information about Grant Rodney Kitchen, please visit:
www.gkspeaking.com

RECOMMENDED READING

THE BOOKS THAT INSPIRED ME TO WRITE *THE DREAM*:

The Power of Now: A guide to spiritual enlightenment by Eckhart Tolle (Yellow Kite, 2001)

A New Earth: Awakening to your life's purpose by Eckhart Tolle (Penguin, 2005)

The Alchemist: A fable about following your dream by Paulo Coelho (HarperCollins, 1995)

The Pilgrimage: A contemporary quest for ancient wisdom by Paulo Coelho (Harper Thorsons, 1998)

A Pilgrim's Guide to the Camino de Santiago: St Jean – Roncesvalles – Santiago by John Brierley (Camino Guides, 2009)

No Boundary: Eastern and Western approaches to personal growth by Ken Wilber (Shambhala, 2001)

A Brief History of Time: From the big bang to black holes by Stephen Hawking (Bantam, 2011)

The Paradox Process: Creative business solutions...where you least expect to find them by Derm Barrett (Amacom, 1997)

Become a Key Person of Influence by Daniel Priestley (Ecademy, 2010).

INDEX

Note: page numbers in **bold** refer to diagrams.

GRANT KITCHEN´s actions speak for themselves.

After completing the Camino de Santiago, an 800-kilometre walk, Grant resigned his successful career as a corporate soft-skills facilitator in Sydney, Australia, and 'began again' in Germany with his wife, Magdalena.

In the six years since, Grant has achieved remarkable results. Not only has he integrated into a new country and culture, he's established his own successful Business English and soft-skills training company and built an incomparable reputation for achieving measurable and practical solutions in the field. He has facilitated over fifty programmes to eleven German multinational companies in English and German, and has employed two facilitators and administrative support.

Grant's courage, tenacity and sacrifices have allowed him to realise his dreams and more. His infectious 'can do' attitude has also helped corporate and personal audiences around the world to reach for the stars and realise their dreams.